Banned in Boston

Memoirs of a Stripper

An Autobiography By

Lillian Kiernan Brown

ISBN: 1-4107-6809-0 (e-book)
ISBN: 1-4107-6808-2 (Paperback)

Library of Congress Control Number: 2003095171

This book is printed on acid free paper.

Printed in the United States of America
Bloomington, IN

Edited by:
Sharon E. Cobb

1stBooks – rev. 09/10/03

Acknowledgments

To my editor Sharon Cobb and Shirley Jordan both fellow Pen Women. Sharon who got the T's crossed and I's dotted so expertly, Shirley who found 1stBooks for me, and to their Penquin husbands, Phil and Joe who read the book and liked it.

DEDICATION

To my husband Jim Brown without whose love and help

this book and my life would not have been possible.

Foreword

It is indeed a great pleasure and honor to write the foreword for this exciting and impressive work, *Banned In Boston..* Lillian Kiernan Brown is to be commended for producing this very readable book on the extraordinary art of Burlesque.

While its origins in America date back to the end of American Vaudeville, burlesque developed in much the same fashion of entertainment as vaudeville, gradually phasing over to a theatrical environment. Although it was Greek inspired, England is credited with burlesque being popularized as early as the 1600's. This set a pattern of an acknowledged art by 1927 at the Lincoln Theatre in London. It was often billed as the 'Beggars Opera.'

When Abie's Irish Rose closed in 1928 after a six year run at the Republic Theatre the Minsky Brothers took over the theatre and converted it to a Burlesque House, the first such establishment on 42nd Street. The Theatre reopened February 12, 1931 with Minsky's production of Fanny Fortsin from France, starring Gypsy Rose Lee. The three strippers most closely associated with the New York theatre were Ann Corio, Margie Hart, and Gypsy Rose Lee.

In September 1935, the city of New York, in answer to many complaints from merchants and civic groups, successfully closed all burlesque theaters in New York, and at the same time banned the use of the Minsky name and the word "burlesque."

Over the years, history of three burlesque queens has remained. Life stories to be visited are those of Ann Corio, Gypsy Rose Lee and Lily Ann Rose. In 1947 the Sally

Keith Revue featured the beautiful, and sexy Lily Ann Rose. This book will reveal the many events, such as being accused of Lewd and Lascivious conduct, resulting in Lily Ann Rose, along with other strippers being arrested and banned in Boston.

Florenz Ziegfeld legitimized Burlesque when he introduced the stylish Gypsy Rose Lee as a headliner in the Ziegfeld Follies. Lily Ann Rose was also a headliner because she was beautiful, talented, and innocent. She wanted to be a star, and she was. She was booked into the same theaters with the great burlesque troops of the day, which included renowned burlesque comedians. The burlesque comedian was always referred to as a "banana" with the lead comedian being "Top Banana." The term "top banana" entered common usage as a result of the 1951 Broadway production by that name, starring Phil Silvers.

Lillian Kiernan Brown is a close and treasured friend of mine. She is warm and loving. She is a fine wife and mother. She is a credit to her profession of journalism. She is an outstanding member of her community, and at the age of 15 the Watch and Ward Society banned her in Boston. She was a Burlesque Queen!

The Lillian Kiernan Brown that I know is a fine writer and organizational leader. She was a chartered member of the Ocala Branch of the National League of American Pen Women where she served as Treasurer and President of the branch. She was Letters Chairman for the Florida State Conference held in St. Augustine, Florida in 2001. She is president-elect of the St. Johns River Branch of the National League of American Pen Women. Lillian Kiernan Brown is a tribute to all women who strive to succeed in a competitive world.

She is real, she is warm, and she is wonderful....

Chris Costner Sizemore Ocala, Florida December 27, 2002

Author of Final Face of Eve, I'm Eve, and a Mind of My

Own.

Prologue

A dear friend and astrologer Jeannette Oswald prepared my Aquarian horoscope recently. She wrote, "The stars were in your favor the day you were born. Because your sun was in Aquarius you were destined to be bright, unusual, and able to work with concepts and ideas. With your sun in Saturn older people will always like you. You were born to accomplish a great deal. Your Capricorn ascendant promises you will be a late bloomer." I had spent my youth struggling to be an early bloomer and had failed. In this book, I will share the memories of those struggles with you.

The 1940's were an incredible time. World War II had just ended when I entered show business. Soldiers and sailors were returning home, marrying the girl next door, starting families and buying homes on their GI loans.

Television had just been invented. Americans were enthralled with the new little box with a black and white screen that brought pictures into their living rooms. Live theater, especially burlesque, suffered from the decline that started with the entrance of that box. Television offered the baggy pants comics a brand new media. Variety and comic formats of early television provided a natural transition for Uncle Miltie, Jack Benny, Sid Caesar, Burns and Allen, Jimmy Durante and many others. But there was no place for the dancing girls who paraded provocatively down strobe lit runways. The years of theatrical entertainment that was Burlesque, a phenomenon unlike anything that had ever existed in show business before, was about to come to an end.

Stripping was an art form. The burlesque stripper was not just a sex symbol. She was a consummate artist. She was never vulgar nor obscene. There was no need to be. A true strip tease artist knew the secret of capturing a man's attention. Her greatest asset was a man's imagination, and she knew how to make it work for her.

I am often asked what those days were like. The music, dance, and entertainment of that era is looked upon with increased nostalgic interest. Very little has been written about it as an art form. I will touch on the legends of burlesque and shatter the mystique. I will introduce you to many of the famous and not so famous burlesque queens whom I got to know while I was in the business. I want you to see how hard they worked at their craft and how much pride they took in what they did. You will discover that these beauties were more than sex objects. They were women who honed their craft and often paid a high price socially and personally for a chance at stardom.

You will meet the people along the way whose admiration somehow made it all worthwhile. The super stars of burlesque like Ann Corio, and Sally Keith who were secure enough in their own work to help me fulfill my dreams of stardom. Funny lady, Totie Fields, who nicknamed me the home body and joked about it. There was Jack Kennedy who would one day become President of the United States, a young handsome Robert Goulet who sang for me as I paraded the stage, and champion boxer, Willie Pepp, who thought I was the most beautiful girl he had ever laid eyes on and who helped further my career. I got to know them and many more like them. I hope I can make you love them as I did.

But there were also some heartbreaking and frightful times in my life when as a teenager. I was raped by the man I trusted most, escaped from the vice of the Chicago mob, was banned in Boston, and thrown in jail for lewd and lascivious conduct. All of this before I was out of my teens.

Occasionally when I hear "A Pretty Girl is Like a Melody," for a brief moment I feel myself getting ready to go on. Burlesque will always be in my blood. I may have been Banned In Boston, but if everything goes as I have planned, I will sure as hell be a star again in heaven.

Lillian Kiernan Brown

Chapter 1
Scollay Square

Boston's Scollay Square was deserted at nine o'clock in the morning on June 1st, 1947. World War II was won and sailors in bell-bottomed trousers no longer swarmed the square. As I walked alone on Hanover Street, I caught my image in the window of Kane's Clothiers. I was satisfied that the lavender tube top and body-hugging slacks fit perfectly on my grown-up, 14 year-old body. I was proud of my big white teeth and smiled often. My mother, Margie's, blue eyes and Aunt Lillian's long thick chestnut brown hair suited me well. I was twelve-years-old the first time I noticed my resemblance to them, my two beautiful mothers.

1

It wouldn't be long now before Lillian Margaret Rose a.k.a. Lily Ann Rose followed in their footsteps and broke into the wonderful world of burlesque.

The Old Howard Burlesque Theater loomed like a dream on my left. The Casino Burlesque Theater marquee on my right announced "Peaches Queen of Shake," but I imagined it said "Starring Lily Ann Rose,"in lights and bold letters. It was there that I wanted to be, but my blonde bombshell mother, Margie, danced in the chorus of that theater and, although I looked eighteen, I was still six months from turning fifteen.

The John Hancock Building in Boston was the weather predictor for the city. When the pointed tower on the tip of the building was blue, it meant the sun would shine. If it was flashing red, you knew to wear galoshes or snow boots. This morning I was out of school and from the window of the fifth-floor walk-up I shared with my grandmother, I saw that the light was blue. The long hot Boston summer of 1947 had begun early. The newspaper announced that Harry Truman was vacationing in Key West, Secretary of State George Marshall addressed the alumni of Harvard University and outlined his plan for European economic recovery, and an ad for warm weather appetite's read "Mevrakos Kool Kandies/Take some home every week / $1.00 a pound."

Everyone in those days dreamed of a home with hot running water, an electric refrigerator, a television set on which to watch Uncle Miltie and imagined an air-conditioner. Some dreamed of owning a $7,000 home in Florida, $50,000 in the bank and retirement. However, those were far from my dreams. I longed to be on stage like my mother and aunt, the LaMont Sisters. I longed to be a star.

Every summer the neighborhood kids would gather in my basement and perform the plays I wrote, produced, directed, and starred in. Now I was 14 years-old. I was grown up and no longer would I dream about being a star. This long, hot summer of 1947, I was going to be a star.

There it was, the Casino Theater. I shifted the weight of the make-up case I had stocked with rhinestone studded net bra and panties, a pair of over-the-waist opera hose, and high-heeled silver dancing shoes, equipment I had been gathering since I was three, and pushed open the stage door. I felt nothing but confidence because almost since the day I was born, I have spent every moment learning to sing and dance. My mother would come home between shows and teach me all the songs and dance steps she knew. She even taught me to read music. What she neglected to teach me was the heartbreak that comes with real life. I was about to learn that on my own.

The doorman at the Casino Theater did his job well. It was imperative that he knew everyone who entered the theater, and as I approached, he looked me over. I smiled, and he knew why I was there. He rang the bell, and I entered a backstage heaven. I went directly to the stage manager, Ed Ryan, whom I had known since I was a little girl since he's married to my Aunt Karin's best girlfriend. "Give me a chance in the chorus. I can sing, dance, and act, and I will succeed." I knew not to plead.

"Okay," said Ryan, "Let me see the legs."

I raised my pant leg and stuck out my right leg for him to see. I may have been dumb and naive but I was not one bit bashful.

"Great legs! You are hired," Ryan said. "Twenty-five dollars a week, 3 shows a day, 4 on Friday and Saturday. Sundays off." He sent me to the captain of the chorus girls to be taught the routine.

"Success! I had been hired as a chorus girl at the Casino Burlesque Theater in Boston, Massachusetts. Very soon now," I thought, "Lily Ann Rose will be a star."

For two days I walked on a cloud. My professional theatrical career began with the captain, Honey Vargas. Honey was a tall, buxom, bleached blonde who was made captain because she had been there the longest. To a naive fourteen-year old, Honey was old, at least thirty, but everyone who was associated with burlesque in the 1940's knew Honey Vargas. She was the one third from the left and every man who ever attended a burlesque show recognized her.

"Parade step, count, one and two and three and four; stay in step with the music." Honey took me under her wing. She taught me in just a few minutes all the steps in the numbers. I caught on fast. They were easy steps because dancing was not one of talents of the chorus girls at the Casino Theater. All they were required to do was parade and look pretty. Most of the girls were faded beauties and most all the numbers were parade numbers which were simple walks in time with the music. The prettiest and youngest girls like Barbara English, June Kiley, and me were spotlighted so it took just a few days before I was selected to do a solo. Indeed, it was the following Monday that the producer chose me for that solo. I was fitted into a sheer costume with lots of sequins. Honey placed a huge feathered headdress on my long, golden-brown hair. I was to perch atop a gold pedestal with my arms outstretched and

7

draped in glittering rhinestones while a male tenor sang *A Pretty Girl Is Like a Melody* as the showgirls paraded around me. Rehearsals went smoothly.

Opening day, I sat in the dressing room with a dozen other girls, sewing beads on a new costume, deep into my usual stardom dream. The dressing room became quiet – I was alone. The chorus girls were in place in the wings. The violins in the orchestra began the intro to the number. I sang to myself – "A pretty girl is like a melody." Then I heard it. The male tenors voice – Oh no! I jumped out of my chair and ran up the spiral iron staircase to the wings. Breathless, I watched, the red velvet curtain open. The girls were parading and the tenor was singing to an empty pedestal. I lost my opportunity, my big break that I had been dreaming of all my life. I would soon be 15 – too old. Life was unfair. I had daydreamed away my chance to be a star.

Chapter 2
Peaches, Queen of Shake

I stood in the wings of the Casino, sunk in the depths of humiliation and despair, when I felt the warmth of her arms around me. Peaches Queen of Shake, the star of the show, had the warmest hazel brown eyes I had ever seen. Her hair flowed down her back in a soft golden blonde wave and formed a high pompadour frame around a soft, white face that glowed like an angels. Her eyes were heavily shadowed in blue and her cheeks were rouged a soft pinkish red.

No one except the stage manager and light crew was allowed on stage or in the wings while Peaches was performing. The rules were strict, absolutely no chorus girls and no strippers. Her act was the best-kept secret since the atomic bomb, but here she was holding me as my heart broke after losing my chance to be a star on the stage in the Casino Theater.

"What's your name honey?" she asked in a soft voice.

"Lily Ann Rose," I whimpered. "I was going to be a star and I missed my cue. I was daydreaming in the dressing room and the curtain went up without me."

"Now, don't take it so hard. How long have you been in the chorus?"

"A week," I answered.

"Look honey, a week is no time to learn this business. Wait until you get years under your nets like me then you'll really know what it is to be heartbroken. Now come on. Cheer up. Look honey, would you like to catch for me?"

"What's that?" I asked and wiped my eyes on the back of my hand smearing mascara across my face..

"When I take off my costume, I'll toss it to you. You catch it and hang it up neatly for me. Can you do that? It'll be a great help. I don't trust any of these girls to catch for me. They'd steal my act so fast I'd get pneumonia from the breeze. How about it?"

"And you trust me not to steal your act?"

"Sure kid, you're still so raw and you have plenty of time to be a star. I'll help you all I can. Now, how about it?" Peaches leaned over to Ed Ryan, the stage manager and said, "Help her out if she needs it. Now, go fix your face. I'm on."

The violins in the orchestra pit started their tune and the lights went down as the first curtain opened and Peaches Queen of Shake stepped on to the stage. She was covered in gold sequins and white net. The crowd clapped and cheered and pounded the floor as she slithered to center stage. As the spotlight hit her she stood still, inhaling the applause. When the second curtain opened, and she threw off a white net scarf readying the audience for what was to come. . The audience went silent while the band played the first four bars of her opening song. This was the first show on Monday morning, and there was a light above the proscenium flashing red.

"Why is the light flashing red?" I whispered to the stage manager. I'd had the terrible thought that the theater was on fire.

"Today is Monday, kid. The city of Boston Watch and Ward censors are in for the first show. We have to keep it clean. No damns or hells in the scenes and no bumps and grinds for the strippers. Get it?"

"I guess so. How do you know the censor is here?"

"The doorman. He controls the light and knows everyone who walks through that door." After Peaches' first rather mild song and dance, the light turned from flashing red to blue.

"Now what happened?" I asked.

"All clear. He's gone, the real show can go on."

On the opening of the third curtain the stage and the entire world belonged to Peaches and she crooned in a soft, sexy voice:

Nuts, nuts, red hot nuts,

The men in the audience went wild, screaming and whistling as she sang as though her song was for each man personally. She peeled off her outer gown of gold sequins, to reveal her body covered in white net and slung her long hair around her shoulders to cover her breasts. Under the lights her skin glowed, white as snow. She had deep dimples in her back and on top of her buttocks. As I hid in the wings behind the curtain, she tossed me her gown. I caught it and hung it up. I was mesmerized by such subtle beauty. Peaches was perfect. But I hadn't seen anything yet.

When her song finished, the orchestra flowed into a slow, sexy tune. She turned her back to the audience and went into her *piece de resistance*, the part of the show she kept hidden from the competition, and the part that made her so popular – her fabulous muscle control. Right bun up, left bun up, down, side to side. Shiver, quiver and shake, all the way up her back her muscles quivered and shook. Her body never moved – just her soft white skin, quivering to the music as the audience roared. It was deafening. "More, more," they shouted and she dropped the net panels that had draped her and tossed them to me. She quivered and shook some more. Then her net bra sailed to me and the audience went wild. The muscles up her back to her shoulders quivered. It was phenomenal. I had never seen anything like it. The band grew louder; the audience pounded the floor, her net panties disappeared and the muscles from her thighs all the way up her back quivered like jelly. There was not an inch on her body that was not quivering.

Then the band played a new song and a chorus sang from the orchestra pit: "Oh it must be jelly 'cause jam don't shake like that." Chanting now, over and over – audience still screaming and pounding for more. I knew then what I had to do. I am going to learn to shake my buns just like Peaches. She was the undisputed Queen of Shake. And to be honest: There never was another one like her.

Chapter 3
General Electric

My missed cue was forgiven. I was on stage. In my naive mind, I was at last a star – my dreams were answered. I now needed to get educated about being a burlesque queen. And boy, did I get an education. I found out very quickly that if one wants to know when the Declaration of Independence was signed or the date of the end of the Civil War, one trots to the closest library. But, if it's a certain gentlemen's worth in dollars right to the bottom line that interests you, or the top stock of the day to buy or sell, one does not go to Merrill, Lynch, Pierce, Fenner, and Smith. No! For the most accurate answer ask a chorus girl. So it was then that Honey sat me down and gave me a sample of her wisdom.

"Lily Ann," she began, "You are going to open up new venues for your talent."

"What do you mean," I asked?

"For example, what are you going to say to a stage door Johnny when he sends a note asking for the pleasure of your company?"

"Well, I could say, 'I like orchids and White Shoulders perfume.' Those things I always have loved. Maybe I'll get them, huh?"

Honey howled with laughter. "Hey girls, listen to this, Lily wants orchids and White Shoulders." The rest of the chorus gathered around and their laughter shook the dressing room. "Boy are you dumb. Did you just get off the boat or what? Haven't you ever heard Peaches sing, 'If I can't sell it,/I'll sit on it,/I ain't givin'/Nothing away.'"

"No, I've never seen Peaches' on stage," I lied, "but if you think I should, I'll be sure to watch her strip next show."

"Oh sure, kid. Don't you know the rules? No one watches Peaches. She's afraid one of us will steal her act. You really are dumb. What do you say girls, let's educate Lily Ann. Okay, what do you want to know first?"

"How do you keep a Johnny from kissing you?" I asked.

"You're worried about a kiss?" Toni Breen jumped in. "A kiss may get you a share or two of General Electric, which is number one on the stock exchange today by the way. When a Johnny asks me what it will take for a kiss, I answer General Electric or AT&T."

"But Toni," I answered, "I don't kiss boys. Oh no! I don't want to have babies." Up until now the extent of my sex education was from Granny's answer to my question on where babies came from. "Boys. Kiss boys, you'll have babies." So when I was twelve, my friend Dolores Rose confided in me that a boy had kissed her. "Oh, Dolores," I said. "You're going to have a baby." She didn't believe me so I told her to ask Granny. Granny did indeed concur that kissing boys made babies, so Dolores and I chose a spot in the basement of our building and fixed a birthing place for her. No birth occurred, but it became our favorite playroom.

My statement on kissing created an uproar in the dressing room. "Did you hear that," said Honey. "I think we got a cherry here. Lily Ann are you still a virgin?"

"Yes. I've never had a boy kiss me. Is there something wrong. Will it keep me from becoming a star?" I was terrified.

"No," Honey said, "But it may keep you from paying the rent."

"But, I live at home. I don't have to pay rent."

"Oh my God, is this kid simple or what," said Honey. "We owe it to the world and to her future to educate her, and now."

Toni said, "Look kid, when you get a note this week, and I am sure you will 'cause you are about the most gorgeous thing this theater has seen in many years, just forget the flowers and perfume shit. Remember this, GENERAL ELECTRIC."

Chapter 4
The LaMont Sisters

The winter of 1933 was long, cold and rainy and our country was in the depths of the great depression. In November of 1932, Franklin D. Roosevelt had defeated Herbert Hoover in the presidential election by promising a "New Deal" and Governor Joseph B. Ely was re-elected Governor of Massachusetts. The working class was hurting, out of work, out of money, out of food. But I was lucky enough to have been born into a family of vaudevillians who were working the circuit and making money. My mother and aunt had a sister act, "The LaMont Sisters."

Aunt Lillian was born in April, 1910, and Margie, my mother, eighteen months later to Italian immigrants in Boston. Their mother, Josephine Johanna LaManna was born in Boston in 1880. Her father was a well-to-do Italian immigrant, Giuseppe Serge, who owned extensive property in Boston's West End. Italians were restricted to the North and West End because the Irish immigrants ran Boston and would not allow them to live in what they referred to as the "Irish white curtain," areas. When Grandmother Josephine's mother died giving birth, her father Giuseppe sent Josephine and her sister to Messina, Sicily to be raised in a convent by Catholic nuns. There my grandmother not only received an education steeped in religion, learned to read and write in four languages, but was given in marriage with a dowry of $2,500 to Pasquale LaManna, a stone cutter and self proclaimed, "Professor of Sculpture." She was fifteen.

With her mother-in-law in tow, she followed her husband to Boston where he lived like a playboy until the $2,500 dowry was gone. In the next twenty years until his death in1915, he fathered thirteen children and carved all the lions in the Franklin Park Zoo and most of the lions and animal heads on many of the buildings built in downtown Boston in the early 1900's.

Granny Josephine was left a widow at thirty-five with eight living children and a few pieces of jewelry from her father's inheritance. Her playboy husband had squandered every dime. But Granny was among the first of the liberated women. She placed her children in the care of her mother-in-law whom she loved as the mother she had never known, and got a job in a sewing factory. She educated her two eldest boys, Samuel and John, who graduated from the prestigious Wentworth Institute. Salvatore enlisted in the

United States Army to fight in World War I. Sam became a journeyman machinist and set out to educate his younger sisters whom all received an education in music and dance. John became a bookkeeper for the Italian Mafia in Boston until 1942 when he joined the Army and fought in World War II.

All the girls, Frances, Jenny, Lillian, Margaret (Margie), and Eleanor wound up in the theater. Frances played the piano for the silent movies. Jenny did a solo acrobat number in vaudeville and died of a ruptured appendix in 1920. When Eleanor, the baby, joined her sisters in show business she selected the stage name of Karin LaNore. Lillian and my mother, Margie who were born eighteen-months apart, were very close and looked like twins except that Lillian had dark hair and brown eyes like her mother and Margaret had her father's reddish blonde hair and blue eyes. They formed a sister act, and at the age of fifteen and fourteen respectively, they joined a vaudeville show and chose a stage name The LaMont Sisters by anglicizing their real name, LaManna. Throughout the 1920's the LaMont Sisters prospered. They sent plenty of money home to Boston to help their widowed mother support the remaining sisters. Granny didn't have to work in the sewing factory any more.

With the Roaring Twenties came sensational events of crime, sex, and sin. Gangsters and bootleggers made big profits defying prohibition. In newspapers across the country comic strips hit full stride and radio was a big craze. Vaudeville and film houses were riding high on the entertainment crest. Women had gotten the vote and were fighting hard to make it on their own. America was at its peak. The Roaring Twenties not only brought prohibition to America but Hollywood thrived and there emerged a glorified variety of celebrities: Mary Pickford, Douglas Fairbanks, The Prince of Wales, Trans-Atlantic Flier Charles Lindbergh, Channel swimmer Ruth Ederle, Prizefighter Jack Dempsey, Footballs Red Grange, the Four Horsemen and home run hitter, Babe Ruth.

It was Christmas 1929 and with the stock market crash in October, a new era was opening up. Soon seventeen-million people would be unemployed. The LaMont Sisters were opening a new show in Buffalo, New York. They were the feature act in the Patent Leather Girls Revue. After four years on the road, Lillian and Margie were seasoned performers. Lillian the silent, raven-haired siren posed for naughty pictures, scantily clad and semi-nude, showing off her shapely legs. Dark, secretive, sensuous, hardworking, she held the act together. Flo Zeigfield was so impressed with her beauty he came backstage one night after a show and asked Lillian to be a Zeigfield Girl.

"What about my sister Margie," she asked?

"Blondes are a dime a dozen, but your beauty is rare. I will feature a number just for you, and I promise you will make big money if you come to New York City with me."

"No thanks, Mr. Zeigfield, I promised my mother to look after Margie. I won't break up the act."

Margie on the other hand was the blonde, blue-eyed bombshell. Being toast of the town was easy for her. She was outgoing, sweet and predictable. Margie wrote the songs and parodies, arranged the music and choreographed the dance routines: "Telling it to the daisies, but it never gets back to you." Sing one chorus; dance two and the third in stop time with a loud finish. For an encore they did, "Just One More Chance."

Always showstoppers, blonde Margie and her dark, sensuous almost twin sister complemented each other with their differences. While Lillian poses in silent beauty, Margie steps into the spotlight and croons in almost child-like innocence;

The object of my affection

That was the very first song Margie taught me when I was three years old. When their show opened in Philadelphia, brother Sam, an engineer in that city, found he had no lack of male friends when his two gorgeous show girl sisters were in town.

While Lillian walked the narrow line of sobriety, Margie fell under the influence of bathtub gin. There was one club date when she and Lillian got into their hotel room to unpack, Margie opened her suitcase to reveal, not one stitch of clothing, but ten bottles of gin for her stingers. This addiction was going to kill her in the end.

I grew up loving my mother, my aunt, my uncles, and my grandmother. I loved all the dancers, singers, and mustached actors that strolled in and out of my homes like a road show. Margie sent packages of exotic gifts and came and went like a soft breeze. All I knew was love and these fascinating show people. Aunt Lillian refused to teach me anything about singing or dancing. "No more show business in this family,' she'd say. "You're going to go to school and be something other than a showgirl. You're going to college."

But when Margie came home for a day or so it was grand. She'd teach me a new dance step or the latest song on the billboard chart, and she always left me a billboard or variety to read. It was the highlight of my life. Every visit was a new adventure, a new boyfriend, a new diamond ring or watch which she usually pawned the next day. There was one diamond ring that Aunt Lil fell in love with. When Margie pawned it, Aunt Lillian's heart was broken, so Uncle Pat, her beloved husband, bought the ticket from Margie and redeemed the ring for her. She loved that diamond ring and wore it until she died at 86 in 1996.

As a child, I remember sitting at Granny's knee while she told me stories about those early days. She respected Margie and Lillian in their chosen profession on the stage. She never really got over the insult of having been "sold" for a mere $2,500. She warned me over and over again, "Don't ever let anyone tell you that you can't do something because you're a woman." And she encouraged me always. "You can do anything you set out to do. But always be careful whom you hurt on your way up because you may meet them on your way down"

She told me she was not allowed into the silent movie theaters where my Aunt Frances, a graduate of the Boston Conservatory of Music, played the piano. Unescorted women were considered "fast women," and were not allowed to enter. Granny said, "I didn't care how fast they thought I was. I went in anyhow." She loved music and the theater and was the first liberated woman I ever knew. She taught me from the age of three to read Shakespeare and all the classics. Thanks to Granny I was three going on thirty. Margie taught me to sing and dance, Granny gave me literary skills and Aunt Lillian and my uncles, Sam, John, and Lillian's husband Pat taught me love. I didn't have the stability of a home base but I had lots and lots of love. There has never been a day in my life that I have not been in love with someone. My mother often told me, "Lillian, you are in love with love." Love has always ruled my life and my heart. The LaMont Sisters continued to work hard, send money home, and hold the act together. Then along came Joseph Rose. This baggy pants comic would do what Flo Zeigfield couldn't – break up the act. The beginning of the end came in late 1931. The sisters were working at the Loew's Theater in Hartford. Margie, who was the better contortionist, was always ready to earn an extra dollar working a side act. In a magic act, she was placed in a crate while the magician thrust swords through the crate. One night, just as the magician was about to release her, someone yelled, "Fire!" The theater emptied but one man had stayed behind and heard Margie's muffled screams from the crate. "Help. Help. Let me out." He released her and from that day forward, second banana Joe Rose was first banana with her. At the moment he saved her life, she fell hopelessly in love. She would not be separated from him. Week after week, month after month, theater after theater, city after city, they played the circuit, and when Margie became pregnant Joe Rose confessed, "I can't marry you Margie, I'm already married."

There was nothing left to say. The LaMont Sisters packed up and left the show to go home to their mother, Josephine's, home in Cambridge, Massachusetts and await the birth together. Lillian was the more sensible of the two girls. She would prepare for the birth like it was her own. "Oh Margie," she would say, "You are so lucky. I'd give anything to have a baby." So in her wisdom she accepted an engagement ring from Pasquale (Pat) De Benedictis. He came from a good working-class Italian family. Granny encouraged her to marry him. "Pat will give you the stability to make a good marriage," she said. The date for the wedding was set.

"Oh how I have prayed to be a wife and mother," Aunt Lillian said over and over to Margie. But Margie thought only of having the baby and getting back on the road with Joe Rose. So it was Lillian who prepared for the child. For four days she stood in a mile long line for a back-breaking job – loading cartons at Schrafft's candy factory in Charlestown. For four days she waited in line with immigrant women who could barely speak English for one lone job that paid eight dollars a week. Lillian, who had been earning hundreds of dollars a week, who was wined and dined by fine gentlemen and scouted by Flo Zeigfield, stood in line for an eight-dollar-a-week job, all for the love of a child that was not hers and was not yet born. After four days, a man walked up the line asking the question of all the women, "Can you operate a machine?" The immigrant women could not speak nor understand English. They just stared at him. When he got to Aunt Lillian she answered proudly and loudly, "Yes, I can." With this hard-earned sweat money of eight dollars a week, Lillian prepared for the new arrival. She bought a bassinet, a crib, a stroller, a carriage, and diapers. She was prepared. She would have a home, a devoted husband, and a child. It was a dream come true for Lillian.

I made my naked debut into this world on January 23rd,1933 in Cambridge, Massachusetts. My mother, Margie looked at me, kicking out like a left-legged dancer and named me Lillian Margaret Rose. She placed me in her sister's arms and went back out on the road with Joe Rose, and Uncle Pat and Aunt Lillian De Benedictis moved me and the whole family to Medford, Massachusetts.

Chapter 5
Hanover Street

When I walked down Hanover Street on that June day in 1947, I hadn't realized I was walking out of the innocent past into the harsh world of reality. Being a star was the only dream I had ever nurtured. So that day I approached the Casino Burlesque Theater, the dreams began to emerge and the past seemed to fade. Down the hill I could see the crossroads where Princeton Street intersected with Hanover Street at the bottom of the hill. Princeton Street was to Boston what Broadway was to Times Square. It was also the gateway to the North End, the Italian district. In the Little Italy of Boston, tenements stood cemented together five stories high, peddlers sold their wares from carts squeezed onto narrow crowded streets, cars honked and drivers begged to get through. Little Italian widows strolled the streets with shopping bags hanging from their black draped arms. Beautiful, melodic Italian music drifted through the air. The voice of Caruso singing vivid Italian arias, and familiar Sicilian folk songs were heard all along the route. Mama, O Solo Mio, and Return to Sorrento made life sensual and musical in a simple setting. Each store was a specialty. A chef cooked pasta in the window of the Prince Spaghetti House and passers by drooled at the spaghetti, smothered in spicy, garlic-drenched tomato sauce piled high on platters. It was Granny's favorite restaurant.

When we lived in Medford, Granny and I would take the electric trolley car and transfer to the subway nearly every day to shop down town. If she needed chicken, we went to a poultry store where live birds were kept in cages. She would check each one out carefully before saying this red hen is nice and plump. I'll take it. The butcher would take it out of it's cage, holding tight to the hens feet as it clucked like a diva in the opera, and with one twist of it's neck, end its life. He would clean it, pluck its feathers and wrap it, feet and all, in brown paper. Granny would cook chicken ala cacciatore that evening. The feet she cooked especially for me. They were my favorite part of the chicken.

Granny said that August is the only month to buy Swordfish, so every August we would take the trolley and subway to the North End, and there, displayed on wooden slabs, were the freshest of the days catch. Italian women walked from table to table examining the fish. Granny would look right into the fishes' eyes. When she decided which one had the brightest eyes, she would make me look into its eyes also. She would point at the fish and say, "there is the freshest, look at those bright eyes." She'd tell the butcher, in English, to slice a big slice right here and wrap it up. Granny refused to speak Italian except when translating for immigrants. She said to me when I asked her to teach me Italian, "We live in America; we're Americans; we speak only English." That slice of Swordfish in August always turned into the best Bracciole Pesce in the world. No one could cook fish like Granny.

Shortly after World War II in 1945, price controls on housing were removed. The Office of Price Administration (OPA) was dissolved and housing was no longer under government control and restrictions. The boys were coming home from their duration and six-month enlistment contract and received 52/20. That translated to twenty dollars a week for one year. They married, went back to school on the GI

Bill and started a family. That created an enormous housing shortage. There were not enough homes to go around.

For Granny it meant the horror of eviction. Her house had been sold and she was given an eviction notice. There was no housing available anywhere in Medford, so we were literally put out on the street. Granny and I moved in with Aunt Lillian, who in all her good heartedness and loving heart offered to take all of us, except the cat, Kutzianna. She would not allow the cat in her house. Uncle Sam refused to part with the cat and moved in as a boarder with a kind neighbor. Uncle John got married and moved in with his new wife and Aunt Karin married and moved in with her new husband. Margie had an apartment in Boston with her third husband, and I alternated between Aunt Lillian, Margie, family, and friends.

When Kutzianna got killed by a car, Uncle Sam decided that the family must be reunited. Margie found us a five-story walk-up cold water flat in Boston's South End. So we packed our belongings and once more, Granny, Uncle Sam, and I had a home together at 181 Shawmut Avenue, one block from Washington Street and the MTA. I could watch the elevated trains from my window. Tremont Street separated just before it hit Shawmut Avenue and went the other way like a V. So one block the other direction Tremont Street had a trolley car line. Shawmut Avenue, like many other streets in Boston was lost in the middle. Boston is truly like its nickname, the "Hub."

As I walked down Hanover Street that June day I had no idea that the innocent past would soon be lost.

Chapter 6

Jack

It was Thursday the fifth of June and I had been working in the chorus of the Casino Burlesque Theater for four days and had gained quite an education from the chorus girls about men. They had me working on a degree in finance and banking – learning how to figure a man's profit and loss statement. Peaches had given me a valuable lesson in muscle control and the art of stripping, but I was confused. As we sat at the long dressing tables, lined with bright light bulbs and looked into the mirrors that we shared, I asked the chorus girls over and over, "Where does love come into this?" I needed to be in love. I needed to be loved. I was sure love, not money, nor stocks and bonds would make me happy. So, when on Thursday night during intermission I received a note in the dressing room – my very first note from a stage door Johnny – I was thrilled. All it said was, "You are beautiful. Anything you want is yours. Just name it." The note was signed Jack with a telephone number to call. I ran all over the dressing room waving the note in the girl's faces. "Look, look," I screamed, "I can have anything I want. I'm going to call him and ask for White Shoulders perfume and orchids."

Honey pointed a bright red, polished fingernail at me. "Wow kid. That must be Jack Kennedy. I heard he was in the audience tonight in Mayor Curley's private box. He is just about the richest congressman in D.C. Kid, you just struck it rich. Forget about flowers and perfume. I told you they wouldn't pay the bills. Get diamonds, jewelry, gold, stocks and bonds, anything but flowers and perfume. When the flowers die what have you got? A bunch of dried up old leaves."

"Yes, but I can press them and put them in the Bible like Granny does." I had an answer for everything.

"Oh my God! She can press them and put them in the Bible. Where have you been all these years, in a convent? Wake up. This is the forties honey. The war is over. Women need to be independent. Take charge. That takes money and brains. Start using your little money maker to get you where you need to go – up!"

"I don't know. I don't think I could ever let a man kiss me if I didn't love him. I can't imagine selling my love to anyone."

"Oh kid, you are hopeless," Honey said and walked away.

I read the note over and over. I remembered Jack Kennedy as he walked the streets of Boston. Up and down Beacon Hill to the South End, the North End and the West End canvassing for votes. Granny and all the family had voted for him. He was a naval hero of World War II. I couldn't imagine any man sending me a note like that when he could have Peaches Queen of Shake or any one in the chorus. Why me? Why was I so special? I had to know. I tucked the note into my net panties and dreamed all night of the handsome Jack who had written and told me I was beautiful.

I got up early the next morning to call the number on the note. A man answered and I asked to speak to Jack.

"This is Jack. Who's calling?" His voice made my knees weak.

"Lily Ann Rose. I received your note at the casino last night. Do you remember me?" I tried to keep my voice from trembling.

"How could I forget you, beautiful girl," he answered. "I won't be in town much longer. Where do you live? I can send a car for you right now. How about it?"

My heart pounded – my mind raced. What'll I wear? What'll I say? What'll I do? What if he doesn't like me? What, what, what? My head was spinning. Jack Kennedy wants me. Jack Kennedy thinks I'm beautiful. Six months before my fifteenth birthday, one week after my debut in burlesque at the Casino Theater, and already I was in love with the most handsome man in Boston, Jack Kennedy." I said. "We have four shows and no breaks. I can meet you after the last show." I was afraid he could hear my heartbeat over the telephone.

"My driver will pick you up at the stage door," he said and hung up.

All day was a blur. I thought the night would never end. Every act, every scene, went on and on. It seemed that every stripper would be on stage forever. I didn't say a word to the girls because I knew they would hound me about stocks and bonds and jewelry. What did they know about love? This man was in love with me. I was in love with him. It would be the most beautiful moment in my life. I knew he would change my life forever. He would make me his own, and I would be his. Jack would carry me away in his big black sedan. What do these chorus girls know about love? All they know is stocks and bonds and a man's financial worth. I have found true love.

After the finale, I slithered into a black strapless dress with thin black straps that crisscrossed over my neck and tied in back. I touched up my make-up and shadowed my blue eyes until they looked like pansies and brushed my hair until it shined half way down my back but left the pompadour that swept up over my arched darkened eyebrows. Gold earrings, the longest ones I could find in my jewel box, dangled from my ears. I left my net panties on and my bra off and rouged the curve of my breasts so he would be sure to notice how firm and pointed they were. I had made a mental note that my breasts were more perfect than the other girls in the chorus. I wanted him to fall in love with me as I had with him.

As promised, the car was parked at the stage door waiting for me when I exited the theater on Hanover Street shortly after 1:00 A.M. My life was about to change. The driver was in front at the wheel, and Jack was seated in back. He wore a big smile and his red hair was short over his ears, long and tousled on top kind of like he had missed a few strokes with his comb. His blue-eyed gaze went through me like an ice pick. I shook as he embraced me and brought me close to him. He kissed me as we rode out of Scollay Square.

"Oh Jack," I cried, "I'm going to have your baby now. But it's all right. I'll have your baby if that's what you want."

Jack glared at me. "How old are you?"

Proudly I answered, "I'm almost fifteen. I'll be fifteen January 23rd."

"Oh my God," he gasped. "You are just a child. I had no idea. Good God, what the hell's the matter with me. You're just a kid."

"No. No." I cried. "I'm grown up. I love you with all my heart. I will be yours forever and ever."

"Oh God," he cried over and over. "Oh, my God."

He opened the sliding glass door between the front and back seats and said to the driver, "Let me out on Beacon Street. I'll get a cab. Then take this kid straight home. Where do you live kid?"

"181 Shawmut Avenue." I sobbed. "But I love you. Don't you understand? I love you. I will always love you."

When the long black car pulled up in front of 181 Shawmut Avenue, the elevator train roared down the tracks on Washington Street high above the Dover Street Station. I felt it roaring at me to shatter my life. I felt like I had lost my chance at life, like it was all over for me. I knew when Jack Kennedy left the car that night he would never be mine. That night I crawled into my bed and cried myself to sleep.

The next day when I went to work at the Casino Theater, I felt like something had happened to change my life. It was like growing up overnight. I was becoming a woman. I didn't tell the girls everything, but I did express my sorrow at not getting what I wanted out of Jack Kennedy, a wedding ring and undying love.

"See," said Toni Breen, "I told you to ask for General Electric." Toni was true to her philosophy. She did marry a millionaire and presumably lived happily ever after.

Chapter 7
Margie

It was Friday night intermission and I had been on stage for five days. Tonight I had been selected as the girl who, between the acts, strikes a sensuous pose as the house lights go up and the candy butchers came down the aisles hawking their wares. The candy butchers were the entrepreneurs of the theater who sold boxes of candy with promises of expensive prizes and pictures of nude beauties inside. It was all a scam, but the crowd loved it.

"Get your candy, get your candy – only twenty-five cents, one quarter of a dollar. Get your candy."

"I got a good look at Joe, the candy butcher, as he shouted the names of the girls in the photos. "Betty Biddle, the bam bam girl, Rose LaRose, Lotus Dubois, sexy, sexy, all in the you-know-what! And that's not all," he shouted, "These boxes hold more than nude ladies. Yes, these boxes contain pictures of some of your favorite Presidents — George Washington and Abraham Lincoln."

A shill in the audience jumped up and waved a five-dollar bill in the air. "I got a president. I got a Lincoln," he shouted and nearly every man in the audience was holding up his money, shouting for the candy butcher to sell him a box of candy. The entire house was in a frenzy for the prize in the box. I moved quietly off-stage, the candy butchers emptied their boxes, the customers emptied their pockets and the house lights went out. The curtains opened, and Act Two began.

This particular Friday evening there was not time to take the subway home for dinner with Granny so I joined the girls for supper at Joe and Nemos. Joe and Nemos club was directly across from the Old Howard Burlesque Theater and all the show people and fans gathered there between shows. Everyone in burlesque knew Joe and Nemos and the walls of the dining room were covered with pictures of the comics and strippers who had appeared at the Old Howard. I hadn't gone there often, and felt tonight was a particular treat – that is until I ran smack into Margie who was still working at the Old Howard. Her blue eyes never left mine as she pulled out the chair opposite me and sat down. Neither of us spoke. All was still except for the hum of the crowd of show girls, a comic or two, and the spectators who came to gape at the girls.

Margie set her stinger on my table and broke the silence.

"Well, little daughter of mine, it looks like you want to be a chorus girl for the rest of your life"

"No," I retorted, "Someday I'm going to be a star."

"Look kid, if you want to be a star this is not the way to go about it. Go home, go back to school and do it the right way. Aunt Lillian loves you and you want for nothing. Why can't you be satisfied with what you have?"

"What do I have?" I cried. "You don't want me, and my father doesn't want me. I need to be somebody. If I don't make it come true, I'll kill myself."

"Ok, Lily," she said. "I can see your mind's made up so look at me and listen carefully. I love you very much, and I want you to be happy and succeed. Just listen and don't roll your eyes at me like I am stupid. I've been around a few years, and I know what I am talking about. Look at me!"

I raised my head and our blue eyes met and in that brief moment I saw a look in my mother's eyes that I had never before seen – pride.

"Sally Keith is putting together a new revue. Go to the Bradford Hotel Ballroom at ten o'clock Monday morning and audition for her show."

"What are you trying to do Mom, get me out of Scollay Square so no one will know you have a grown daughter?"

"No! I am trying to talk some sense into you, and for God's sake don't call me Mom around here."

"Why? Don't you think it's time we had a mother and daughter talk. How am I ever going to learn about men?"

"Don't give me that crap. You're almost fifteen years old, and I'll bet that if I sat you in a corner and had a good heart to heart talk with you, I'd learn plenty. As for the facts of life I'm afraid you're in love with love. You've fallen in love with every singer, comic, and actor I ever brought home. Remember Don Humbert and Del Markee? How about Frank the cop on our beat? You had a mad crush on him when you were six or seven. Yes, Lillian, you are in love with love. The best advice I have for you is stay away from candy butchers. They love to prey on girls like you. And always remember a stiff prick has no conscience."

I couldn't believe what my own mother just said. She thinks I'm a liar. I left the restaurant without eating and ran all the way back to the Casino Theater hoping my tears wouldn't smudge my make-up.

Chapter 8
Sally Keith

Margie's advice stuck in my head. Sally Keith was the most famous tassel dancer of all time. She had headlined at the Crawford House in Scollay Square for the duration of World War II, and her name was always in the newspapers and in Variety and Billboard. Perhaps Margie was right. I was excited at the thought of trying out for the Sally Keith Revue. I couldn't wait for Monday to get here. But what am I going to wear? At home Saturday night I dug through my closet. Nothing! I found nothing good enough to wear for an audition for Sally Keith. I've got to look sexy. I've got to look like I'm on my way to stardom. What to do? Then I thought of Carol.

My friend, Carol had lost her mother, father and only brother to tuberculosis and lived in a tiny alcove in her aunts attic tenement apartment next door. After graduating from high school she got a job in a bank and paid her aunt five dollars a week for the room. She spent the rest on clothes. A look into Carol's closet was like taking a peep into Bonwit Tellers. I ran all the way down five flights and up five flights next door to Carols loft.

"Carol, guess what?" I was breathless from running.

"What? What is it?" Carol asked.

"I'm going to be star." I had to shout in a whisper so her aunt couldn't hear us.

"You're what? Where? How? At the Casino?"

"No, no I am going to be in Sally Keith's Revue. She's auditioning Monday, and I'm going to tryouts. Only one thing is standing in my way."

"What's that, Lily Ann?" Carol was smiling. Not at me, but at my excitement. She was my best friend and knew me better than anyone. "What's standing in your way of becoming a star?"

"I don't have anything to wear. My clothes are all so, you know. They're not stylish like yours. All I have are hand-me-downs from Aunt Karin and school clothes Granny makes. I need something sexy – a showstopper." I eyed her closet.

"You're in luck. I have just the number for you. Just got it out of lay-away at Jordan Marsh – paid a dollar a week on it for thirty weeks. It'll look gorgeous on you." Carol pulled a lavender silk beauty out of the closet. It had wide dolman sleeves, a cape bolero back and was embossed with flowers of gold and green leaves from neckline to hemline.

"Wow!" I stared at it. "I've never seen anything so, so – I can't describe it. It looks like a flower garden in the United States Mint. Know what I mean? Do you think it'll fit me?" I couldn't shut my mouth.

"Try it on. If it fits, you can borrow it."

I scrambled out of my clothes and poured myself into Carol's masterpiece. It fit like it was sculpted to my body. It emphasized my breasts and accented my hips.

"Golly, that dress looks like it was made for you," Carol said. "It makes your waist look so tiny."

"Yes, yes," I shouted. "This is it. This dress will surely make me a star. There'll not be another like it at the audition. Oh, thank you, thank you Carol. I'll pay you back someday, I promise. When I get there I'll not forget my friends."

For the next two nights I tossed and turned in bed, but I was up bright and early Monday morning. I wore silver, spike-heeled shoes that laced up over my ankles with the lavender silk and brushed my hair until it glowed like a chestnut waterfall. I applied foundation and blue eye shadow highlighted with a hint of purple mascara on my lashes. Today is my day I thought.

I was one of the first to arrive at the Bradford Hotel Ballroom. A striking brunette in rehearsal costume and tap shoes accompanied by a gray-haired, skinny, five and a half foot tall man walked up to me, looked me square in the eye and said, "Hello. I'm Pepper Russell, captain of the chorus line and producer of the dance numbers. This is my husband, Murph Rubinstein. He arranges all Sally's music and is her personal drummer."

Gosh, I thought, Sally is the worlds greatest tassel dancer and has her own personal drummer. "It must be great to be star. I'm going to be star someday," I said to her.

"Yeah sure, kid," she answered and walked away.

Girls began arriving. I sat in a chair by the dance floor where I could see everything. I didn't want to miss one beat of the music or one step of the dance. As I looked around the room, I spotted a very familiar face. "Oh no," I gasped. "Aunt Karin." I tried to hide but she spotted me and stomped over to me.

"What are you doing here?" she demanded.

"I'm here to try out for Sally Keith's new revue".

"Oh yeah! Well you'd better get your fanny home where you belong. This show opens in September and the only opening you're going to see in September is school. Now get moving, you hear me?"

Aunt Karin was the baby in Granny's family and got all the attention until I came along. She and I competed for everything. At times she loved me and at other times she resented me, especially when she came home and found I had plundered her room and wardrobe trunk which held wondrous treasures like furs and net lingerie. So when she found me auditioning for Sally Keith's Revue, I was that little brat invading her privacy once more. She wanted me out of her business.

"But I want to be a star," I cried. "I don't want to go to school."

"You know I'm out of work, and I need this job. If I don't work, I don't eat, I don't pay my rent. Get it! I need this job. If you try out for this show, I'm leaving. It's either you or me and you belong in school."

Although we fought like sisters at times, she was my aunt, I respected her and would not argue with her on this point. She needed the money. I didn't."Okay," I squeaked. "I won't try out. But can I stay and watch?"

"Okay, you can stay and watch but keep quiet and then go home."

Just then Sally Keith entered the room. She was as beautiful as her pictures. Platinum blonde hair swept up into a pompadour on each side. Gosh, she must be thirty, I thought. But she looks wonderful for her age. The music started, the girls paraded, and Pepper made her selections for the first number. The first number was to be an Indian dance and Murph pounded out tom-tom beat on the drum. Pepper pulled each girl from her chair and placed her in the circle on the dance floor. My feet were tapping to the rhythm. Pepper walked up to me and took my hand. I looked over at Aunt Karin. She shook her head no. It took all the strength I had to say no, I don't dance. I lied and my heart was breaking.

After what seemed hours, it was over. The girls that were chosen were signed up and given a show-up date. Aunt Karin was among those told, "don't call us we'll call you." The ballroom was empty except for Murph, Pepper and Sally Keith. Sally looked me over and asked, "What about you young lady, what can I do for you?"

I took a deep breath and said, I'm looking for a job."

"What can you do?" Sally asked.

"I'm ah, a, secretary." I blurted out. "Yes, I'm a secretary."

"You know," smiled Sally, "that's just what I need – a glamorous secretary. Here secretary, she said as she tossed me her clipboard with a pencil dangling from it. "Follow me and start secretarying."

The rest of the day was a whirlwind. First there was Sally's car, a gold Cadillac convertible with her initials *S K* painted on the doors. The top was down and the seats were covered in genuine leopard upholstery. Wow! What a dream of a car.

"Secretary, do you drive?" Sally asked.

At five, I had climbed into my Uncle John's car, took it out of gear on a hill and steered it to the bottom. Luckily, the car wasn't going so fast he couldn't catch up with me, jump into the driver's seat and stop the car. He was so scared at what I had done, he promised to teach me to drive

if I would never do that again. When I was twelve, he kept
his promise and gave me lessons in his 1941 Ford coupe.

"Do I drive?" I answered weakly. "Yes, I know how to
drive." But before I could say that I wasn't old enough to
have a drivers license, she tossed me the keys. I got in,
started the dream car, and drove Sally Keith through the
narrow streets of Boston, first to a brief meeting with
lighting engineers, then to Helen's Famous For Costumes
shop. All day I stayed at Sally's side like a shadow, doing
exactly as I was told.

"Secretary," she would say, "get her phone number."
"Secretary, write that date down in my calendar as soon as
we get back to the hotel." We lunched at the Bradford Hotel
on Tremont Street after which I drove her down Boylston
Street past the Boston Common and the Public Gardens and
onto Copley Square. Sally lived in the most elegant

apartment I had ever seen. She occupied the VIP Suite at the Copley Plaza Hotel. I gaped at the gold-domed lobby, the glitter, the antiques. We crossed the lobby and took the elevator to Sally's suite which overlooked Boylston Street and the lush green of the Public Gardens.

The early Boston settlers had the sense to reserve and preserve the beauty of the New England landscape through the Public Gardens. They belong to the citizens of Boston and will be enjoyed by them for centuries. Though I had walked through the Boston Common and Public Gardens hundreds of times, I had never seen them from this height. I was overcome by their beauty and it remains primary in my memories of Boston and Sally Keith.

Sally was amused at my awe over the view and watched me savor the moment then motioned for me to come and sit by her desk. "Secretary," she began, "this job is going to require a lot of your time. Are you prepared to devote yourself entirely to it and to this production from the very first stage, such as we did today, until the moment the lights go on, and we open in September?"

My blue eyes met her brown, and my dreams of becoming a star faded. Could I give them up to be a secretary to a star? I thought for a moment and the answer was clear. "Oh, yes, Miss Keith, I will devote my life to this production. Anything you need I will do. I will fetch. I will. I promise I will."

"Do you think you'll be able to stay here with me during the times we will be working late? And please call me Sally."

"That won't be a problem. I am staying with my Grandmother on Shawmut Avenue for the summer. I live part time with her, part time with my mother and part time with my Aunt and Uncles. I sort of live just anywhere I want. I'll talk to Granny tonight. She approves of what I'm doing so I'm certain it'll be all right."

"Good. Thirty-five dollars a week to start, and I am sure you'll be a fine secretary. I'm going to order room service. We'll have a bite of supper, work on notes for tomorrow, then call it a night. But be back here bright and early tomorrow morning. We have a revue to get on."

Later as I walked home on the streets of Boston from the elite Back Bay to the dingy, South End, all that went through my mind over and over was, somehow, I will be star. I will be a star just like Sally Keith.

I arose early the next morning and told Granny all about my new job. "Granny," I said, "Don't worry about me. I'll call every day. I'm only a short distance – Copely Square."

"Copely Square. You're going high class. Good luck, Lily," she said.

I ran all the way to work that morning and had to awaken Sally when I got to her suite. She didn't look too well, and I recognized the symptoms right away. I'd had my share of experience with too much bathtub gin from Margie. I checked the near empty glass beside Sally's bed and sniffed it. I knew the scent well. "Oh no," I cried out in silence. "Oh no, not stingers. Please God, don't let her be like Margie."

I got Sally stirring and ordered breakfast from room service and after coffee Sally was ready to work. She got out a stack of photos and went over them with me. They were photographs of her triumphant days, and as we looked them over, she told me about them. "I was a winner in the beauty contest in 1933 at the Chicago World's Fair when I was fifteen years old, just about your age. That's where I'm from originally. My father had a bakery in Chicago. You know, you remind me a lot of myself at that age. I had such dreams and hopes. It was there I met Jack Parr."

"Oh, yes Jack Parr," I said, "I remember reading in the Daily Record about you and Jack Parr. It was a big story. I mean when you fired him, he sued you, right?"

"Yes. We had a very angry separation. I'm sorry it ended that way, but I wanted to be free to produce and more or less guide my own career. But I owed Jack Parr a lot. When the judge ordered me to pay him, I did willingly. He was well paid. Jack discovered me when I won that beauty contest at the World's Fair. He approached me with the idea of the tassel dance. He said he could train me to be the world's greatest tassel dancer, and he did. He had the costumes and tassels made and taught me how to use them, but it was me who worked hard at perfecting the act. I gave him all I had and all my living and breathing moments went into that tassel dance."

She held a tassel in her hand, "right tassel right, left tassel left, then right, left, right. Then both right both tassels left. Turn around right butt right; left butt left; then right, left, right. Then both together. There's not another dancer in the world that can twirl tassels like me, Sally Keith. I am the world greatest tassel dancer."

She put the tassel down and continued, "I signed a contract with Jack giving him the rights to twenty-five percent of all my earnings for life."

"Wow," I gasped, "that is a lot of money for a lifetime."

"Yes, it is. At the time I didn't realize what I had done. But I had nothing, so I figured I had nothing to lose. Then one day in the middle of the depression, Jack went to the owners of the Steel Pier in Atlantic City and asked them to feature me in a show. They laughed at him when he asked for two hundred fifty dollars a week 'Are you kidding,' they said. 'Look at this place. We're in the middle of a damn depression. People don't have any money. This place is empty every night. How can we pay two hundred fifty dollars to an unknown tassel dancer when talking picture stars can't even draw an audience? No thanks. We have to decline.'

'Okay, I'll make you a deal you can't turn down.' Jack said. That was the beginning of a new era for entertainers. Jack Parr started it all with just one idea." Sally paused for a moment to catch her breath. "Then Jack said, 'I have Sally Keith, the most beautiful, and greatest tassel dancer in the world. She won the beauty contest at the Chicago World's Fair. I guarantee that she will pack this showroom every night, and if she doesn't, you don't have to pay her two hundred fifty dollars a week. You pay her nothing.' You should have seen their faces light up. You could almost hear them say, wow, what have we to lose? 'But,' Jack continued, 'if she's successful and packs the joint like I predict she will, you'll pay her twenty-five percent of the gross receipts for the length of the contract.' Steel Pier jumped at the deal. Jack drew up the contracts, and the rest is show business history. I packed the place every night and was the longest running act in Atlantic City history. We made a small fortune there and went on to the Crawford House in Scollay Square under the same arrangement. I stayed there for four years, during the duration of World War II. I was the first performer to work on percentage of the house. Jack Parr pioneered that type of arrangement and of course I will always be grateful to him for discovering

me and helping me become a star. But ten years of my life –
I felt that was enough. I wanted and needed to be free."

"Gee, Sally, tell me about this picture," I said holding up
a photo of Sally dressed in a United States Army uniform
which made her look like a WAC.

"Oh, that was taken in Hollywood. I played the part of
Jean Harlow in a movie and appeared at the Hollywood
Canteen for the war effort wearing that uniform."

Then Sally autographed a few of the photos and said,
"When requests for pictures come in send these, they are
my favorites."

"Wow," I thought, "someday I'll be posing for photos
and autographing my own pictures."

Through the summer, each day was a new adventure for
me, and I stayed busy answering Sally's every need.
"Secretary, answer the phone." "Secretary, call Walter

Winchell." "Secretary order lunch." Then one morning as opening night for the Sally Keith Revue approached, I drove Sally to Helene's Costume Shop in the heart of Boston's theater district to select costumes for the chorus girls. Helene brought out costume after costume for Sally to see and touch. After a while it was obvious she couldn't make up her mind. She turned to me and said, "Secretary, how about you trying on some of these costumes and modeling for me. I think I could make a better choice if I could just see them on a person.

I almost ran to the dressing room and tore off my skirt and sweater and squirmed into a scanty two-piece, skin tight, dance costume of black satin. Tiny straps over the shoulders held up an equally tiny green-sequined bra. I entered the room with the parade step I had learned at the Casino Burlesque Theater in those two weeks. I used all the drama of a showgirl that I could muster stretching my legs to show them off and walked with what I hoped was confidence and glamour. I kept going back to the dressing room, changing and re-entering in character of the costume I was wearing. In about an hour Sally had made the selections for the show.

On the drive back to the hotel she asked, "Secretary, with a body and talent like yours, why do you want to be a secretary?"

"I have a confession to make, Sally. I am not a secretary. When I came to the auditions in June, I came because I wanted to be in your show. I want more than anything to be just like you."

"Well, it's about time. Why did you wait so long to tell me? Now the show is all cast and in production. Why didn't you try out at the auditions?"

"My Aunt Karin LaNore tried out for your chorus. She was there that day, and told me how much she needed the job and if I tried out, she wouldn't. So I didn't try out. I stayed to watch and when you asked me what I did, the first thing that popped into my mind was secretary. I'm sorry I lied to you, but I wanted to be part of your revue. I'm really and truly sorry. Please forgive me. But I've learned so much over these last six weeks it has been heaven for me."

"Lily Ann," Sally said as she reached over and wiped a tear from my cheek, "I've grown to love you like a daughter. First of all let me clear one thing up. I know your Aunt Karin, she is a wonderful girl and a very talented dancer and acrobat. But, we were looking for chorus girls who will mix and drink with the stage door Johnny's. Your aunt doesn't drink, smoke nor mix with gentlemen. She is strictly an entertainer. There is no way we would have hired her. So don't feel guilty. You'll not keep her from working. You've been an enormous help to me, and I'd like to teach you everything I know and make you my protégée. What do you say I change your name from Secretary to Protégée.?"

"Oh Sally, I don't know what to say. I'll try hard to be just like you, and do everything you say. I promise."

"I know you will." Sally assured me. "You learned to be a good secretary in such a short time."

"I can thank Granny and my teacher, Miss Griswold, for that. Columbus School didn't have the books needed to feed my appetite for reading, so every day I'd walk home with Miss Griswold, and she'd lend me a book. The bond between us grew so in third grade when I sang in Hansel and Gretel, Miss Griswold sat in the front row and applauded the loudest. In sixth grade, I wrote a play in honor of my teacher's birthday, and Miss Griswold arranged for an empty classroom for me to present it to the entire school. After I left Columbus School, I didn't see her again until ninth grade when I was told I wouldn't graduate until I'd finished my Home Economics assignment. I hated sewing so I took the apron home and asked Granny to finish it. She refused."

"I'll be here to help," she said. "But you must do it yourself. I will not sew it for you."

I went to Miss Griswold crying with frustration. She sat down beside me as she always had when I needed help. "It's important you at least try to do the things you don't like to do. Remember that not everything in life comes easily on the first attempt. Don't be afraid to fail. Above all don't fear rejection and always do your best at anything you do. Now let me see that apron."

"It had taken her nine years to teach me to be my own person and to do it myself no matter how difficult the task."

"You're a lucky girl," Sally said. "We all should have such good mentors."

On returning to the hotel, Sally placed a call to Pepper Russell and Murph to come to her suite as soon as possible. We went to work as soon as they arrived. Together they worked out a Hawaiian number for me for the finale. The song was *Blue Hawaii* – followed by the beat of Murph's drums and the *Hawaiian War Chant..* They also decided to include me in one of Sally's numbers, identically costumed with flowers on my bra instead of tassels. The flowers were sewn on strategically to go around like the tassels as I shook my shoulders. I caught on fast and in no time I was turning those flowers like a seasoned trouper. Sally and I worked the number where I was to follow her and shadow her every

83

move. We named that the Shadow number. We worked on those for days and when we had it perfected, I knew my dream was about to come true. Lily Ann Rose would get billed as a special attraction, Sally Keith's Protégée.

Chapter 9
Sharples and Naples

Now in rehearsal, the show was coming together. The comedy team of Sharples and Naples was on stage one afternoon rehearsing lines and picking chorus girls to work on the very funny sketch, *The Politician.*. I was in the audience to get a glimpse of Charlie Naples, the little baggy pants comic who I had heard was a brilliant master of comedy and a small version of Jimmy Durante. His straight man, Wally Sharples, was a big, well-dressed, well-groomed, handsome man who used his weight to intimidate the little comic. Every time Charlie Naples spoke a line, I laughed. I couldn't stop laughing at this funny little man being picked on by this oversized straight man. I couldn't control myself in this almost empty showroom.

"Just a second." Charlie stopped the rehearsal. "Who is that little doll making all that noise out there?"

"I'm sorry," I said. Charlie came down stage to get a good look at the giggler who had managed to upstage him.

"That's okay, that's okay," Charlie said. "Come up here, I want to get a good look at you."

As I approached him, I was still laughing uncontrollably. Soon, the entire cast was laughing with me. Charlie didn't stop the laughter. He didn't say a word. He squinted at me then looked toward Wally. Each time he moved he got funnier, and I laughed all the harder. After a few minutes of this hysteria, he asked again, "Who are you, kid?"

"I am Sally Keith's protégée. I am going to be in the finale."

"Kid," Charlie said, "can you learn these lines? There are just three: "I took my father's hat to the cleaners and they lost it." "I took my father's shirt to the laundry and they lost it." "I took my Father's pants to tailor's and they lost them." Only three lines and I'll ask Sally if she'll let you do all three lines in the scene. You'll do them all instead of having three different girls do them. We'll have just one "talking woman." What do you say, will you do it?"

I was still laughing but managed to answer. "Sure, I'll do it if Sally will let me." I ran back stage to Sally's dressing room, breathless with excitement. "Sally, I already know my lines and Sharples and Naples want me for their "talking woman." Can I do it, please can I do it?"

"Sure, protégée," she said, "Now let's find a costume for you to wear. It's got to be a knockout."

We headed straight to the wardrobe room, and there Sally found a tight fitting black one-piece strapless dress. I slipped into it and hurried back to the stage. Charlie gasped. I heard him whisper to Wally, "She's beautiful. Now if she'll just learn her lines."

*Charlie Naples wrote all of the scenes done by the comedy team of Sharples and Naples. During the research for this book I learned that Charlie Naples had died in about 1994 and when my attorney contacted the attorney handling his estate he was told that all Charlie's work was in his head and there was no written work left. I have written this scene from **The Politician** from memory in memory of its creator Charlie Naples whom I consider to have been the funniest comic in Burlesque.*

The Politician

Set: A backdrop curtain of a city street, storefront, with a street lamp and a fire hydrant.

Cast: Charlie Naples as the aspiring politician, Wally Sharples as his wise cracking campaign manager, Lily Ann Rose as the damsel in distress. Enter Sharples followed by Naples looking around, The audience is the crowd that has gathered to hear the political promises:

Sharples: Okay, Charlie here we are. Start addressing this crowd.

Charlie: *Looking around sheepishly*: If you elect me to your town council I promise to. . .

*Lily Ann Rose as the woman enters and begins to weep interrupting Naples. He looks at her bewildered.***Sharples:** Well ask her what's wrong, Charlie.

Charlie: What's wrong young lady why are you crying?

Talking Woman: "I took my father's hat to the tailor and he lost it." *I tried to cry, but I couldn't. The moment Charlie Naples looked at*

89

me it was all over. I held my hands over my eyes and again laughed insanely. Charlie milked it for almost ten minutes.

Sharples: Well Charlie, if you want her vote you better give her your hat.

Charlie: My hat?

Wally: Yes, your hat.

Charlie hangs his head and hands the girl his hat. She runs off stage.

Charlie: *Continuing his speech.* If I am elected to your town council I promise I will . . .

Lily Ann Rose enters again, crying. Charlie tries to ignore her but can't.

Wally: Ask her what's wrong Charlie.

Charlie: *Looking bewildered.* What's wrong young lady?

Talking Woman: I took my father's shirt to the laundry and they lost it.

Charlie: *Looking at Wally annoyed.* What should I do?

Wally: Give her your shirt.

Charlie: Give her my shirt?

Wally: Yes Charlie; give her your shirt. You want her vote don't you?

Charlie removes his shirt and hands it to her reluctantly, and is left in his undershirt. The woman runs off stage clutching his shirt.

Charlie: *Again addressing the audience*: If you elect me to your town council I promise I will. . .

Talking Woman returns crying. Charlie is really shook up and with a little banter and help from Wally, he is urged to ask again although he doesn't want to.

Charlie: What's wrong young lady, why are you crying?

Talking Woman: I took my fathers pants to the Tailor's and they lost them.

This time Charlie is beside himself, the audience is roaring: everyone knows what is about to happen. Charlie tries to get out of this: He argues with Wally for a while and when the audience is convinced that Charlie

91

will give his pants to the damsel in distress he yells:

Charlie: Okay smart guy if you think she needs a pair of pants so badly give her yours.

*He rips the pants off Wally Sharples, and the straight man is left standing in a loud pair of shorts and then – .***Black Out**

Intermission

Lily Ann Rose in her favorite pose

Aunt Karin LaNore

Aunt Karin LaNore

It was cold. My cheeks were red and stinging. I could not feel the tip of my nose: I breathed hard as steam puffed from my nostrils. I did not dare open my mouth for fear my tongue would freeze. It was truly a cold New England December day. I was eleven years old and the year was 1944. Just six months earlier in June, Uncle John had survived the Allied invasion of Normandy. He had been in the battles for North Africa, Sicily, Italy, and France. We knew he was well because we were still receiving those precious little V-mail letters from him. Uncle Sam was working hard on the home front on the twenty-four hour production lines at General Electric. I did not know what he was building there because everything was kept secret as the BIG war was still being fought all over the world. Our meat ration was two pounds weekly and the cat got most of mine because he would not eat a thing but beef stew and I did not like meat. I guess that is why I was so streamlined and he was a big, fat, gray tabby. Aunt Karin had named him Kutzianna.

Aunt Karin had moved into Uncle John's room for the duration so I ran upstairs as fast as my legs would carry me, two steps at a time, and made a mad dash for her room. I loved Aunt Karin's room. Not so much for the room, but for the treasures that it held.

Aunt Karin was the youngest of the girls. She was born Eleanor LaManna in 1914 just before her father died. Uncle Sam did his duty as the oldest boy to educate her and paid for her lessons at the Mary V. Corbett School of Dancing. Her graduation recital was held in Shuberts Lyric Theater in Boston, June 9th, 1930. When Aunt Karin joined her sisters in show business she selected the name of Karin LaNore.

Aunt Karin was the baby of the girls who were all in show

business. Jennie who died from a ruptured appendix in

1922, Frances, who mastered the piano in vaudeville and

movie houses, and Lillian and Margie. Yes, Karin was the

baby until this little brat; Lily Ann Rose came along and got

all the attention. Aunt Karin and I competed for everything

and at times she loved me and at other times she resented

me. She was especially resentful when she came home to

find I had plundered her room and her wardrobe. It was

those times when she would really light into me.

During the war Aunt Karin worked at the Casino

Burlesque Theater, the Old Howard, and the Gaiety. At

times she moonlighted at a graveyard shift assembling war

materials in a factory. She had had an unhappy marriage

and was divorced in 1939. That is when she moved back in with Granny.

So, that is why when she found me auditioning for Sally Keith's revue, it was that little brat invading her privacy once more. And that is why she wanted me out of her business.

But, what I remember most about Aunt Karin was her incredible musical talent as a whistler. She whistled like a sacred instrument the songs of her times.

"The Indian Love Call,"

sounded the most beautiful when Aunt Karin put her bright, red, cupid-doll lips together and blew incredible, almost symphonic music into my life.

The LaMont Sisters

left to right: Betty, Mai, Lilly, Edna, Freddie, Patsy, Tina,

Marge, Jennie, Harriette

Patent Leather Girls with Lillian and Margie

Margie with some of the Patent Leather Girls outside a
theater in Buffalo, New York. Circa 1928

Margie LaMont

Lillian LaMont

left: Ann Corio at the Old Howard

right: Ann Corio

Ann Corio

The most beautiful woman in Burlesque was without a doubt Ann Corio. Not only beautiful in body, Ann Corio was talented, sweet, and caring. Ann Corio was the woman I most admired while growing up in the thirties.

Granny loved her too. And of course the fact that she was an Italian didn't hurt. Granny loved burlesque and took me every week to see the show at the Old Howard. Margie, my mother worked the chorus of the Old Howard so I spent a lot of time backstage.

Margie's favorite story about me was the time Ann Corio came home to a delicious Italian dinner at Granny's. She told the story so many times that is why I have such a vivid memory of it.

While everyone was sitting around after dinner enjoying an Italian coffee flavored with a hint of Uncle Pat's home-made Anisette, I quietly sneaked into Aunt Karin's bedroom and scuttled around in her wardrobe trunk. I knew my way around it well because it was a regular habit when she was not in her room.

I dressed in her flesh colored net panties and rhinestone bra, covered myself in white ostrich feathers and smeared my lips with her reddest lipstick and came out with my impersonation of Shirley Temple singing: Good Night My Love: Only it came out Goodnight my Wuv because I still could not pronounce my L's yet. After all I was barely three years old.

Then as I proceeded to strip naked, Granny whisked me up and carried me to my bed. But I don't think Ann Corio ever forgot me.

Because, after making the movie White Cargo, with Buster Crabbe she returned to the stage as Tondelayo. In the 1940's when I was about ten years old during World War II she appeared in person at the RKO Theater in Boston. I skipped school to see the show.

She was as beautiful as I had remembered her when I was three years old. I recall her act as Tondelayo. She wore a sarong and did a Hawaiian dance and a very funny monologue during which she flubbed a line. Then ad-libbed, "I better watch myself or I will wind up back at the Old Howard."

I will never forget that day. After the show I went back to the stage door and sent her a note. She sent for me immediately and in her dressing room we talked about the "Old Days." Then she took me to lunch at the Stage Door Restaurant.

After that she wrote me and sent some beautiful autographed photographs. I treasured them for years.

I tried hard to emulate Ann Corio and many of my early photographs resemble her early photographs.

Ann Corio without a question is, and always will be Queen of Burlesque.

Boston

I love Boston. Let me tell you a little about it so you will have a true picture of Boston, Massachusetts.

When the colonists first arrived in Boston in 1630 they had no idea they were mapping out a city of historical landmarks for generations of Americans to venerate.

With freedom most in their minds they had the foresight to set aside a center of the city that it's citizens could always enjoy. They named the two sites, The Boston

Common and the Public Gardens. Nearly all the main streets in Boston are laid out around them so all streets, north, south, east, and west lead into the hub of the city. But, in doing so they made it easy for generations of history minded tourists to find their way around a city full of old world history and New World construction. Walking the two-mile long Freedom Trail in Boston takes a full day but the visitor experiences some of our country's most hallowed landmarks.

It is best to start at a central location. Find the Boston Common. A bold red stripe on the sidewalk leads visitors on a walking tour of Boston's historic sites.

Unfortunately Scollay Square was demolished in the 1960's to make way for progress. The Old Howard Burlesque Theater and the Casino Theater are both gone. But you can walk down Hanover Street to North Street and the Paul Revere House. Surely you remember Paul Revere who waited in the Old North Church for the signal that warned the British are coming. "One if by land, two if by seas." He made the famous ride to Concord and Lexington calling the Minutemen to arms starting the Revolutionary War.

Boston is also famous for serving a great pot of hot tea, baked beans, fresh seafood caught daily in Boston Harbor and authentic Italian delicacies found in the North End.

When you have finished walking the narrow streets of Boston you will have lived through nearly 400 years of history. The contrast between the narrow crooked streets of historic Boston, winding past Revolutionary Shrines, hallowed churches and the modern streets of today will forever be etched in minds and hearts as a genuine symbol of honor to embrace forever.

I guess that is why those of us who have been Banned in Boston, understand why we were banned and are not ashamed but proud of our heritage.

left: Rocky Marciano

right: Jimmy Sauer

This photo taken October 30, 1951 Marge LaMont wrote:

"This is the line at the Old Howard

(One girl is not here she was upstairs smoking)

left to right back row

Lola Marsh, Lorretta West, Mattie Mixon, Toney Loup

Barbara Louden

Front row sitting;

Babs Johnson, Marge La Mont, Terry Mixon and Ruth

Morgan

Missing is Pearl Johnson, and she is pretty too."

Marge LaMont and Clicker Joe having dinner in Joe and Nemo's?

(not documented where this photo was taken) between shows at the Old Howard

Rocky Marciano and his sparring partner backstage at the Old Howard in about 1951 when Marciano was striving

to make ends meet as a boxer before winning the World
Heavy Weight Championship.

During World War II Uncle Pat served in the United
States Coast guard and was stationed in California. During
that time he rekindled the burlesque and vaudeville
friendship with Lou Costello and he was a frequent guest at
the Costello home. They had a lot in common, They both
loved to eat good Italian food and Uncle Pat loved to cook.
He was at home in Costello's kitchen. Uncle Pat told us
that, "Lou Costello loved Uncle Pat's roasted chicken in
wine and baked lasagna."

Sally Keith

Shadow

Hawaiian Number

Statue

Margie

Jennifer

Lillian and Margie

1920's Mystic River Beach

Karin

Lillian

Aunt Lillian: Naughty, Naughty

In the 1920's

Bud Abbot

Lou Costello

Uncle Pat with Lou Costello

Official Universal Studio photo

Released for publicity in 1944

LaMont Sisters

Margie and Lillian

Granny

Granny

Without Granny there is no LaMont Sisters or Lily Ann Rose. Granny was and still is the "Star of the Show." For without her love for her family and wisdom shared with all she met, life would have been very empty. So this book would not be complete without a tribute to Granny

Granny was born Josephine Johanna Serge in Boston, Massachusetts to a rather wealthy Italian immigrant in about 1880. Her mother died giving birth to her sister four years later so as a result both were sent to Sicily to a Catholic Convent to be raised and educated. It was a harsh existence for the girls but they got well educated in reading, writing, history, and four languages. No love: But Granny managed to save all her love to disperse to all she came in contact with for the rest of her life.

Her wisdom came in spurts such as: "Be careful of whom you step on your way up. You may meet them on your way down."

"Don't kiss boys: You'll have babies."

"Never fight with your husband. Keep peace always. When he tells you what to do, say yes dear. Then do what you wanted to do anyway."

Once in 1935 or '36, during The Great Depression when jobs and money were hard to come by Granny and I was sitting on the porch under the beautiful spreading oak tree that covered the three-story house. A neighbor, Senora Lucia came running by, out of breath yelling, "Mrs. LaManna, Mrs. LaManna, come hurry, come, they are giving away free flour and butter down at the fire station."

I was sitting at her knee and looked up, my blue eyes glowing, "Oh Granny, butter real butter, you know how I love butter, hurry, hurry, let's go get the butter!"

"Lily," she said as she crossed her arms over her full-breasted homemade house garment. "We live in America, we are Americans, and we do not take charity, we give charity."

It was always that way. Granny found ways to be a good American by giving to others, even if it was just writing a letter for those who could not write, or interpreting a letter or legal paper. Granny was always willing to help others.

"Always be kind to animals." There was always a flock of birds following us wherever we went. The Boston Commons was a favorite spot in the spring and summer. Together we spent hours spreading stale bread that we carried in our shopping bags by electric rail and subway to Boston just to feed the pigeons.

At home in Medford under the old oak tree there were always flocks of birds waiting for Granny.

Granny had auburn hair, light brown eyes and beautiful smooth light olive skin. Her husband Pasquale La Manna had red hair, blue eyes, and a red handlebar mustache, which gave their children a mix of dark and light complexions and blue and brown eyes. Lily Ann Rose got Margie's blue eyes and Aunt Lillian's dark hair, which was the combination of granny and Grandpa. Somewhere she got Granny's literary talent and her ability to love.

Granny had learned to love her mother-in-law like the mother she never knew and always instructed me this way, "When I die, bury me in the family plot but not beside my husband, Pasquale. Bury me beside my mother-in-law."

Granny is buried in Malden, Massachusetts, beside her mother-in-law, as she desired. What more can be said about Granny's ability to love. How many women do you know will request to be buried beside their mother-in-law?

This photo of Lily Ann Rose was one of Granny's favorites

Lillian LaMont

Dawn, Charmaine, and Lily Ann

A way out of Chicago

Lily Ann Rose

Lily Ann at Lake Geneva

Lily Ann at eleven years old

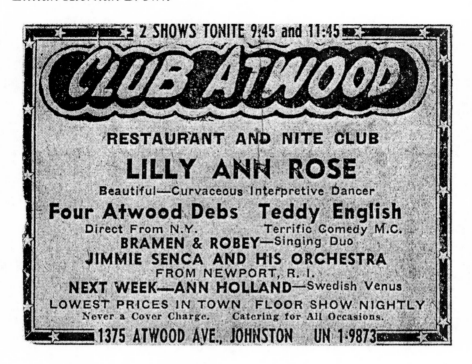

A clip from the Club Atwood in Rhode Island

Lily Rose

Where can I find my Lily Rose? Do you know my Lily Rose?

You know the young pretty girl with bright blue eyes and Roman nose.

I once saw her on Broadway. She smiled at me: She sang for me:

I remember tearfully, how love flows as she sings, La Vienne Rose.

No: that's not my Lily Rose

You don't know my Lily Rose.

Where can I find my Lily Rose? Do you know my Lily Rose?

I once saw her in Chicago; she danced like a Zephyr in the wind, her long, raven hair floated behind on the clouds. She was alone in the cold, growing old.

No: That's not my Lily Rose

You don't know my Lily Rose.

Where can I find my Lily Rose? Do you know my Lily Rose?

I once saw a lone black cat, watching over her, loving her:

She lay still: Tears fell from her paled eyes: Her skin had turned to ashen gray and her raven hair had turned to silver: A shroud covered the scars on her body:

Only the handprint on her face was visible.

Does your hand fit the mark?

Did you put it there?

No: That is not my Lily Rose: You don't know my Lily Rose.

Where can I find my Lily Rose? Do you know my Lily Rose?

I once looked up to the heavens and there I found my Lily Rose.

Goodbye she whispered through the sea, I must leave you now for I hear My Grandmother calling me.

My tears for you are real: For it is your loss when she goes.

Only I shall find my Lily Rose.

Because you are one of those who don't know and never

knew my Lily Rose.

Chapter 10
Opening Night - Loss of Innocence

Opening night was only a few hours away. I left the showroom and went home to have lunch with Granny. She gave me her blessings and wished me luck. I was in my glory. The last words I said to Granny that afternoon before I left were, "Don't worry about me Granny. I will be good, and I'll always remember what you taught me, to always try my best to do what is right."

I bounced down the five flights of stairs and down Shawmut Avenue to catch the Dover Street train. The roar of the trains that ran high over the streets of Boston was just another sound in the everyday life of a native. I stopped long enough to give Ida, the newspaper lady, the change from my pocket as I usually do, and said, "I'm in a big hurry, Ida. It's opening tonight at the Bradford Showroom and I'm Sally Keith's protégée."

Ida sold newspapers from her wheelchair day after day. She greeted me with a smile, "Ah, my Rose in the gutter," she would always say and kiss my hand "I'll read about you in the Daily Record, hey?" Ida laughed.

"Yes," I said, "Look for my picture in 'Along the Hub Rialto.'" Both of Ida's legs were missing from the knees down and life was not easy for a cripple selling newspapers for pennies on the streets of the South End. Someday, I promised myself, when I am a star I'll do something nice for Ida.

Before I reached Dover Street station, I ran into the cop on the beat, Frank Gates, one of Boston's finest. Frank was tall, handsome, and brave and I had known him since I was a little kid. Every summer when I came to stay with my mother on Shawmut Avenue, before Granny moved there, I would walk the beat with him, holding his hand. He'd call in on the patrol box on the corner, and say, "See you, tomorrow kid," and leave me there. I looked up to him like the father I never had. I loved Frank with all my young heart. He was my hero and when he told me stories about his father, a policeman before him and a sergeant on the Boston Police Force, I was enthralled. When I was thirteen, I had confided to Frank that I'd never been to a circus. Granny would never take me because she felt they were too dangerous. Many children had been kidnaped and many circus tents had been destroyed by fire over the years. So the summer after I turned thirteen Frank bought two tickets to the circus playing at the Boston Garden. He asked

Granny's permission to take me. Granny gave in mainly because he was a police officer, and she felt I was safe. Frank was the only man in my life other than family that I truly loved and everyday I told him so. Frank would smile that handsome Irish smile and say, "Someday Lily Rose you'll meet a man that you really love and I'll be just a memory."

"No," I would pout, "I'll always love you."

So it was a very happy moment when I ran in to Frank on the way to my big night. I could share my good news with him.

"I'm getting off duty," Frank said. "Come with me. I have something I want to share with you."

"I'd like to, but it's opening night, and I must be on time."

"Come on Lily. This really means a lot to me."

"Where are we going? I have things to do before opening. I'm really going to be star, Frank. Just like I always told you."

"Let's go someplace private. I'm in uniform so we can't go anywhere where we'll be seen, understand? I promise I'll get you to the Bradford on time for the opening show."

"Well, okay," I said. I'd have trusted Frank with my life.

When he led me to a damp basement apartment, I frowned. "Whose place is this?"

"It's my buddy Eddie's place. He's on another beat on Dover Street. You know him, they call him Soupy because his name is Campbell. Come in here. I want to talk to you." Frank pulled me into the one bedroom apartment, put his arm around me, and unbuttoned my top button. I was horrified when he pulled off my blouse, unsnapped my bra, and pushed me onto the dirty, crumpled bed. He crushed me under his six-foot frame, yanked my panties to my ankles, and straddled me as he pulled off his uniform, the blue of Boston's finest. He crushed his lips to mine – not with love, but with fierce, possessive passion.

I turned my face away from his lips and cried out, "Please, no, Frank. Please no. Don't do this. I don't let boys kiss me. I'm a virgin. Please Frank." I pleaded, "What'll I tell Granny?" But my pleading went unheeded. He pushed into my body. I screamed. "You're hurting me! Stop! It hurts!" But he wouldn't stop, and in a few moments it was over. Frank collapsed on my body, breathing hard as he cried. I held Frank in my arms for a few moments, and we cried together.

"It's time to go," Frank said, "I promised you'd make it to opening night on time. Get up."

I pushed myself from the bed, pulled my panties on and fastened my bra. I felt dirty. There was a smear of blood on my underwear. I hurt all over. This was not the circus. This was hell. I was so numb I couldn't cry as we walked to Frank's car. We drove in silence on the short trip to the Bradford Hotel. I opened the door of the old Ford sedan, stepped out onto the curb, and stared at Frank hoping for a word that would ease my pain. My eyes pleaded for an answer. Why did this happen? Raped by a Boston police officer that I loved and trusted. No, this can't be happening.

"Please Frank," I pleaded, "look at me. Tell me it's alright. Tell me you love me."

But all Frank said was, "You can't tell me you were a virgin, Lily."

I was numb from pain when I entered the Bradford Theater on opening night. I hurried to my dressing room not looking at anyone or anything. I was ashamed and disillusioned and my body felt strange and dirty. It didn't belong to me anymore. There was a stranger lurking in there. I hadn't even stopped to look at the life-size poster of me that Sally had put up in the lobby that read:

FEATURE ATTRACTION LILY ANN ROSE

SALLY KEITH'S PROTÉGÉE.

I showered, and scrubbed until I was sore and put on an extra heavy coat of pancake make-up, darkened my eyes 'til they were blue-purple and waxed my lashes long and black, black, black.

That night on stage Lily Ann Rose was the funniest "Talking Woman" Sharples and Naples had ever worked with in "The Politician" scene with those three lines, "I took my father's hat to the tailor and they lost it: I took my father's shirt to the cleaners and they lost it: I took my fathers pants to the tailor's and they lost it'. They milked the audience for laughs so long, Lily Ann Rose got a standing ovation. The only difference was, tonight, when I had to cry out my lines, "I took my father's hat to the tailor's and they lost it," I didn't laugh. I buried my face in my hands and the audience laughed alone. They didn't know that my tears were real.

Chapter 11

Shadow : A Star Is Born - the Child in Me Dies

During the last few days Sally had costumed me in some of her tailor made gowns. In the poster photo, I wore a white satin fringed skirt with matching long fringed gloves and bra. It was the gown she had selected for the "Shadow" number that we had rehearsed for tonight's opening. It was the poster of my dreams. I was at last going to be a star and Frank had stolen what should have been the happiest hour of my life. The entire evening was a blur.

Sally, who came into my dressing room just before the show, knew something was wrong – that I was not myself. "What is it Shadow, what happened?"

"I can't tell you." It was all I could say.

"Well get over these first night jitters. We have a full house – a lot of important people are out there, including Mayor James Michael Curley. So, snap out of it quick. This is your big chance."

Murph and Pepper came in to find out what was wrong, but I wouldn't talk about it. I could only mourn. How could Frank do this to me? How can I tell anyone? How can I tell Granny? When the music began for the "Shadow" number I was ready, but I made a promise to make Frank pay for what he had done to me. I also promised to forgive him but to always remember this night. Granny had taught me to forgive, but never forget.

Sally came in and dressed me to perfection. She knew just how to drape the white satin band around my breasts so it would fall perfectly when the parasol was drawn across my chest and my left arm was outstretched. We had rehearsed it to perfection for days. The number went like this: Sally strolled on stage in a magnificent white satin gown and white parasol both accented in white fringe. I followed Sally dressed exactly like her. Every move she made, I mimed in precision. The white of the gowns under the twin spotlights reflected the blue of the strobe lights and shone directly on us as the music played:

"Me and my shadow."

Through the pain of humiliation, I followed Sally just as we had rehearsed. Then came the moment to place my right hand holding the parasol over my breast while the fringe that had been covering my breasts fell to my feet with my left arm outstretched. Only this time I put both the right hand with the parasol and my left arm out. The fringe fell and exposed my breasts with pink nipples standing out for the entire world and Boston's finest to see.

The roar of the audience was deafening. I stood frozen. Sally looked back over her shoulder and realized what had happened. She had been upstaged by her protégée. After our bows, she grabbed me by the arm and yanked me into the wings. I was mortified – Sally was furious.

I followed her backstage pleading, "Oh, Sally. I'm so sorry. It was an accident. I didn't mean it. Please believe me."

When we got to her dressing room she said, "Are you real or just putting on an act? I have to get ready for my number, and you have to change for the finale. We'll talk about this later. But I warn you if you did this on purpose, you're through as my protégée. Get it! I will not stand to be double-crossed. Now get out of my way." Sally reached for the stinger sitting on her dressing table.

By second show time the house was packed full, and there was a waiting line to get in. Sally demanded that I stand frozen like a statue during the "Shadow" number – she needed time to decide what to do. The audience clapped and yelled, daring me to move, but I obeyed Sally's instructions. The Hawaiian number finale was fine because under the blue black of the strobe light all that was identifiable was the crimson glow of the flowers on my breasts and hips and the green glow of the grass skirt. The rest of me showed only black. As the flowers twirled they appeared to be floating in a black dream cloud but the rest of my body remained frozen like a statue. The applause was deafening. But I knew I was in big trouble. What a nightmare of a night. I had notes waiting for me in my dressing room from the audience requesting me to come to their tables, but Sally wouldn't allow me to leave the dressing room until she got to the bottom of my brazen act.

By the close of the second show Sally was loaded with stingers so it was not a good time to discuss my predicament. She needed me to drive her to Jimmy O' Keefe's for a late night supper and a spot on the late night radio show to plug the show's opening. Jimmy O'Keefe's was in the theater district next door to the Schubert Theater and a very popular place with celebrities and visitors. Sally had enough stingers in her to forgive and forget, at least for the moment. She was treated like royalty at Jimmy O' Keefe's – best table in the house, service fit for the Queen of Tassels, and a prime rib so thick and huge that it fell over the edge of the platter.

Steve Allison was the host of the all night talk and music show broadcast from O'Keefe's. Besides playing music, he interviewed all the celebrities who had shows along the Hub Rialto. Because she was so inebriated, Sally sent me up to the microphone to say a few words about her new revue. I apparently spoke like I had been on radio all my life because the phone started to ring and caller's questions and comments poured in. I got up to leave but Steve held my arm. "Lily Ann, stay. We've never had a night like this. No one has ever generated so much interest. Please, stay a while longer." I stayed all night and by sign off, I had learned the ropes. Steve got up to take a break and visit with some of the celebrities and left me alone with the engineer. I think Sally was beginning to have second thoughts about canceling me. The publicity I was generating was valuable and by the end of the show, Allison had asked me to come

back and be a regular.

Chapter 12
Red Light

It was 6:00 in the morning, before I took Sally home and caught a taxi. I stopped at the twenty-four hour Emporium, a drug store with a lunch counter where show people met for every reason, breakfast, lunch, dinner, a ride, or just hoping for an agent to offer them a club date. I bought a bottle of the darkest, black, hair coloring I could find, and got back into my taxi. From there, I could see the top of the John Hancock Building. The red light was burning. It meant a stormy day for Boston and, as it turned out, for me.

I trudged up the five flights to Granny's tenement and straight into the bathroom where I tore open the bottle of black hair dye and poured it over my head, working it into every strand. I wanted my hair to be as dark as my heart. It took only a few minutes. I rinsed off the excess color, dried my hair, wrapped it in a towel turban, and walked into the hall. I picked up the telephone on the long marble table in the dark hallway.

"Devonshire 0584, please hurry."

"One moment, please."

My lips were quivering. I was dry and parched.

"It's ringing. Margie, please answer."

"Hello," a sleepy voice answered.

"Mom, it's me Lily Ann. I have to talk to you. It's urgent. I need help."

"What is it now Lily Ann? What have you done?"

"Oh, it's awful. My life is over. Sally gave me a chance and I missed my cue." I began to sob.

"Calm down and tell me what you did. I am sure it is not the end of the world."

"Last night was opening night and I was doing my feature number, you know, *Me and My Shadow*. Oh Margie, it was awful."

"Come on, Lily. Nothing's that bad."

"Wait 'til you hear. I had this beautiful white satin parasol in front of me, and I was draped in a white satin and fringe with Sally's white fox wrapped around me. I was supposed to parade behind her and do everything she did. It all went well until the last four bars. I was supposed to put the parasol over my head, bring my left arm across my breasts, and loosen the fringed bra. Then, as it dropped, I was supposed to bring my right arm holding the parasol in front of me and watch the bra drop to the stage. But I got so flustered at all the screaming and clapping. I loosened the bra and flung both arms out and there I stood, bare-breasted. Oh Margie, it was awful when Sally grabbed me by my arm and jerked me into the wings. She was livid – accused me of stealing her show." I sobbed into the phone. "But, I truly didn't mean it. It was an accident."

"Lily Ann, stop crying and listen to me. It sounds like you're creating another scene."

"No. No, Margie, I am not making this up. I did it. It happened just like I said. I up-staged Sally Keith."

"I know you, Lily. You are an inveterate scene maker. You remember that scene you created when you were about three-years-old? That strip you did for Ann Corio."

Except for my mother and Aunt Lillian, Ann Corio was the show woman I most admired and imitated while growing up. Besides being one of the most beautiful woman in Burlesque, she was talented, sweet, and caring. Granny loved her too. Of course, that she was Italian didn't hurt. One day when I was about three, she came to Granny's for an Italian dinner and while everyone was sitting around after dinner enjoying an Italian coffee flavored with a hint of Uncle Pasquale's home-made anisette, I sneaked into Aunt Karin's bedroom, scuttled around in her wardrobe trunk put on a pair of her flesh colored net panties, a rhinestone bra, covered myself in white ostrich feathers, and smeared my lips with her reddest lipstick. I pranced into the room and went into my impersonation of Shirley Temple singing *Good Night My Luv* (it came out *Goodnight My Wuv)* and performed my best strip. Before I got down to the altogether, Granny whisked me up and carried me to bed, and I don't think Ann Corio ever forgot me. After she made the movie, *White Cargo*, with Buster Crabbe, she returned to the stage as Tondelayo, and in the 1940's, when I was about ten years old, she appeared at the RKO Theater in Boston. I skipped school to see the show. She wore a sarong, did a Hawaiian dance, and a very funny monologue during which she fluffed a line and ad-libbed, "I better watch myself or I'll wind up back at the Old Howard." After the show, I went back to the stage door and sent her a note. She invited me into her dressing room, and after we talked about the old days for a while, she took me to lunch at the Stage Door restaurant. Later, she sent me a note telling me that Boston is her favorite town and gave me some autographed photos which I treasured for years until a boyfriend of Margie's stole them from the mantle. I tried hard to emulate her and many of my photographs resemble her early photos. Ann Corio is without question the Queen of Burlesque.

"Yes, Mom, I remember," I said. "My first strip. I wanted to be a star like Ann Corio."

"So Lily Ann, you're just running true to form. This thing can't be as bad as you're describing. Go to bed and get some rest. Things will look better when you get up. Go to work tonight and do the best you can do. I'm sure Sally will see it was an accident. Now hang up."

"Bye Margie." I walked back to my bedroom, and looked out the window once more. The light was still glowing red atop the John Hancock Building. I was alone, and I had failed again. I walked down the long dark hall to the kitchen where I fell to my knees in front of the brand new gas stove that Uncle John had just purchased for Granny. I opened the oven door, turned the gas on, laid my face on the oven door and gave up. Just then I heard Granny's footsteps down the hall. She'd been hanging laundry on the roof and I thought, oh my God, what am I doing. What would this do to her? I jumped up, closed the oven door and turned the knob to off.

Granny came in the door carrying a clothes basket. "What do I smell?"

"Nothing, Granny. It's nothing."

I slept very little that day. The phone rang off its black cradle, and Granny did her best to answer all calls. One was the Post Master's Union wanting me to do a special show for their upcoming banquet. They had sent an invitation by special messenger, but Granny wouldn't let him in. She locked the front door which was usually left unlocked all day. After all, there were five tenements in the old brick brownstone.

The afternoon edition of the Boston Record published a photo of me under a headline which read: "Lily Ann Rose

Banned in Boston." Hours before the show was to start, lines formed for tickets. The response was phenomenal. But this was not to be my ticket to stardom. Boston's Watch and Ward Society had sent a representative to the Bradford Showroom with a very firm message – "We will have an officer in the audience for every show and if Lily Ann Rose dances on this stage tonight or any other night, she will be arrested for lewd and lascivious conduct and the entire show will be closed."

Chapter 13

Black, Blue and Green - Theodore That Is

I was jolted awake sometime during the afternoon by the doorbell ringing off the wall. "Okay, Granny," I muttered, "I'll go down and answer it." I threw on a robe wrapped a towel around my dyed hair, hurried down five flights of stairs and flung open the door. There he stood, immaculately dressed in a gray suit, a tie, top coat, and a very expensive wide brimmed gray felt hat. He had a spray of orchids in one hand and a ribbon wrapped bottle of White Shoulders in the other. He looked me square in the eye and said, with great authority, "Theodore Green at your service mademoiselle."

"I don't give a damn. Who you are. What do you want?"

"I want to talk to you Lily Ann Rose. It is very important."

"I've had a long, hard night, and I don't want any club dates or private shows so go about your business. I'm tired and have a show to do tonight."

"I know," he said and took a step toward the door and handed me the perfume he'd brought. "That is why I am here. You need help. I know what you're in for, and I want to be your friend. Can I come in?"

I searched his face for a reason to say no, but only saw that his gentle green eyes held a look of genuine kindness. "Come on in," I said and locked the door behind him. "It is a long way up." I didn't know it then, but this was the beginning of a friendship that lasted for many years.

Granny was in the kitchen when we got there and Theodore presented her with the orchids and kissed her wrinkled hand. "Theodore Green, at your service Senora," he said.

Granny's eyes shone and her sigh told me that Theodore Green had touched her heart.

"Granny," I said, "Mr. Green is here to help me with the pickle I got myself into. Isn't that what you said, Mr. Green?"

"Please, call me Teddy."

I pulled out a kitchen chair. "Sit down Mr., I mean Teddy."

"Would you care for a glass of wine or a cup of coffee?" Granny offered and set an ash tray in front of him.

"No gratzi." he said. "I don't drink or smoke. May I call you Granny?"

"Of course. All Lily Ann's friends call me Granny. I have some pasta fagiole on the back of the stove, Mr. er Teddy would you care to join us for supper?"

"I'd be delighted." Teddy Green said and settled into an old wood oak chair where he soon would be a fixture. While Granny set the table, tossed the olive oil mixture into the fagiole, and made a fresh pot of Italian coffee, Teddy and I had a long talk.

"Lily Ann," he began, "You are in for a long siege from friends and enemies now that you have been banned in Boston."

"What do you mean? Not many know about this incident." I said.

"The Watch and Ward Society has placed a ban on you and when they get through with you, young lady, you'll be notorious. Wait'll you read the Record today. Everyone will know. I'm here to be your friend and protect you from harm."

"Why are you interested in protecting me?" I was thinking about a policeman I thought would protect me from harm but hurt me more than I had ever been hurt only twenty-four hours ago. My life was changing much too fast. I took the towel off of my hair and my dyed black hair fell down around my face and shoulders. It was as black as my heart felt.

"Because," he answered, "I know what it means to be persecuted by the law and hounded by the press. I've spent years behind bars for mistakes I'd made and for some for which I was innocent. I want to be your friend. I want to help you."

Granny served the food on her best china, and we sat around the old oak table and ate, dunking bread into her delicious Italian coffee. Granny liked Teddy from the beginning. I could tell by the way she waited on him, and smiled as they talked. And I could feel the friendship and camaraderie from this stranger who stopped his life for me, a struggling dancer, who wanted more than anything in the world to be star in show business. "Why me?" I asked again.

"Like I said," he answered, "I've seen you on stage and I've grown to care about you and want to help. I know what the police can do to a person's life, and I don't want it to happen to you."

"In the last twenty-four hours, my life has changed more than I can tell you. I accept your help and friendship." Then I hugged Teddy Green.

He bent down and hugged and kissed Granny on both cheeks and said, "Granny that was the best pasta fagiole I have ever eaten," and slipped a crisp one hundred-dollar bill into her apron pocket.

Teddy Green became one of my best friends, always at my beck and call over the next few years. Granny, of course, loved him and decided somehow he was a salesman for LaTouraine Coffee. I don't know whether Teddy told her that, or she'd just imagined it. When my friends asked Teddy what he did for a living he always answered, "I rob banks." I never believed that, and it always got a big laugh until once, several years later, he was in Chicago on business and a police man asked him what he did for a living.

"I rob banks," he answered. This cop believed him and arrested him.

Theodore Green it turns out had committed the Norwood Bank robbery, the largest robbery in Massachusetts' history.

While serving his 160 years in the Massachusetts State Prison, he was instrumental in saving the prison guards who were being held hostage for weeks in a prison riot. Following that, he was sentenced to Alcatraz for the remainder of his sentence where he studied law, asked for a new trial, and got his sentence overturned. He was released and, as a free man, spent the remainder of his life as a spokesman on the perils of a life of crime.

Chapter 14
Madam Kazaza

"Shadow, what did you do to your hair?" Sally screamed when I walked into her dressing room. She was seated at her dressing table, the vanity lights shimmering on her blue eye shadow and platinum blonde pompadour. She jumped up and grabbed a handful of my hair and shook it in my face. "What did you do, and why the hell did you?"

"I dyed it as black as I could get it." I wanted to cry out and tell her it's now as black as I felt inside. I wanted her to hold me like a daughter and feel sorry for me. I wanted to tell her about the rape and how Frank had taken advantage of my devotion to him. But I couldn't tell anyone. So I just said, "I thought black hair would look more authentic for the Hawaiian number."

"Well for God's sake get rid of it." she yelled. "Next time consult me before you do something so dumb. Why would you mess around and ruin a good thing? Start washing it out immediately, you hear?"

"Yes, I whimpered. "Sorry, I didn't mean to upset you."

"We'll talk about it later. Right now, we have more urgent business. The Watch and Ward Society has notified me that if Lily Ann Rose dances on stage tonight or any other night, she'll be arrested for lewd and lascivious conduct. They've posted a police officer and a censor on the premises for each show. So until this whole mess dies down, we have to outsmart them. First, I've added another sketch to Sharples and Naples which you'll do with them. And in the Shadow number you will not, and I mean not, move, you hear! I said, do you hear? You can talk, you can pose, but you will not dance."

"Yes, I hear you. What do I do?"

"When the curtain opens on the Shadow number you'll be standing center stage like a statue, fully clothed in your costume. You will remain in that pose – S T A T U E – get it? Like a statue – while I do the number. We've shortened it to a four-bar intro and one chorus. Now, go find Charlie and rehearse the new Madam Kazaza sketch. Everything else stays the same, and the finale is all done in strobe so the censors won't even know you. Now get moving, and let's hope we can keep it clean."

By this time the lines had formed out of the lobby into the street around the Bradford.. The entire town wanted to see the stripper who was banned in Boston. Naples and Sharples were waiting for me in their dressing room. We went over the sketch, and I learned Madam Kazaza's lines in about five minutes. The sketch went like this:

Madam Kazaza

Wally Sharples introduces the **World's Greatest Living Mind Reader, Madam Kazaza.**

Enter: *Madam Kazaza carrying a crystal ball – very sexy – not too much on the body but a scarf dangling off her hair and lots of rhinestones on her neck.*

Madam Kazaza : Good evening.

She wiggles a bit and puts her hand out for Wally to kiss.

Sharples: I hope you're ready for this audience tonight, Madam. It looks like a tough one.

Madam: I'm ready. She pulls the scarf around her eyes like a blindfold.

Wally steps down stage into the audience and walks to right stage and takes an object from a man in the audience.

Sharples: Madam, I have in my hand an object. Can you tell me what I am holding? Be careful don't let this one stick you!

Madam: A stickpin.

Charlie in the audience right stage begins to heckle

Wally: Oh for cripes sake. *The audience begins to howl at the obvious clue.*

Sharples: I have an object in my hand, Madam. Watch out this one may stump you.

Madam: She struggles a bit then says: A watch.

This goes on throughout the entire sketch. Sharples and Naples go at each other, all ad-lib. The audience is with Naples all the way as he heckles them as phonies. The sketch ends leaving the audience in stitches and bow after bow for Sharples and Naples and Madam Kazaza.

After the show, we went to Jimmy O'Keefes where Steve Allison was waiting for me to do my guest spot on his radio show. I was told there was a celebrity waiting to meet me. Walter Dropo was the Red Sox Rookie of the Year and had been in the audience and sent a note backstage, but Sally hadn't allowed me out of the dressing room. So he came to O'Keefes where all show people meet after their show on the Hub Rialto. Allison introduced us and asked if we'd have a conversation on his show. We agreed and the conversation turned out to be all about baseball and Ty Cobb. I had my Uncle Sam to thank for any knowledge I had on that subject. After the show, Dropo said how nice it was to meet me finally. I told him it was my pleasure. Then he left with another show girl. I felt I had been dumped. I was sitting all alone at the desk listening to the music that was being aired when another man sauntered over and introduced himself. "Hello, you look like you can use a friend. I'm Milton, Walter Dropo's brother."

"I'm pleased to meet you, and yes, I really can use a friend. I'm a little surprised that your brother walked out on me the way he did. But I guess men do things like this. That's what makes a dog man's best friend. A dog wouldn't do that."

"You sound like a dog lover. You must have a good one." Milton said.

"My dog Queenie died a few years ago, and I'm finding out that she was the only real friend I've had that I can trust. I miss her more tonight than I ever have."

Gratefully, two o'clock in the morning came around very quickly. I drove Sally to her suite and caught a cab home. I tried washing the black color out of my hair before I went to bed but it didn't do much good. It was going be to a long black road ahead before my life or my hair lightened up again. But as I lay in bed that night summing up all I'd been through in the last forty-eight hours, I was grateful for one thing. The chorus girls at the Casino Burlesque Theater had taught me a lot in the few weeks I was there. First, I'd learned that you didn't have babies by kissing – you had to do a lot more. And they shared with me the secrets of not getting pregnant. Frank had done at least one thing right that terrible day. He didn't release himself inside me. I guess I can thank my stars that he was a good Irish Catholic.

But being banned in Boston was not what I had imagined my career on the stage would be, and I wished in vain it had been different. The next morning, the doorbell awakened me, and I jumped out of bed. The sun was shining in the dormer windows and the light atop the John Hancock building was blue. It was going to be a good day. I threw a robe on and ran down the five flights of stairs. I opened the door and Milt Dropo stood holding the cutest ugly Boxer puppy I had ever seen.

Oh, what a darling," I gasped.

Milton put the puppy in my arms. "It's for you. My brother Walter and I want you to have it. He's sorry he ran off on you last night and hopes this pup makes up for it a little."

"Thank you Milt, I love it." I took a quick glance at her bottom and said, "I'll call her Princess. Oh, thanks, she's wonderful. Come on up and have a cup of coffee."

So Milt came up, had coffee, and Granny gained another fan – another friend. Everyone to ever meet her became her fan. The five flights of stairs one had to climb to visit with her were like an ascent to another world. Granny's kitchen was the closest to heaven that a person could get. Princess cuddled up at her feet and life was again complete.

Chapter 15
Love and the Old Ball Game

When I was growing up, baseball players loved the fans as much as the fans loved the players. My Uncle Sam had aspired to be a baseball player and still loved baseball. He loved to tell baseball stories and in me he found a willing listener. He said that Ty Cobb is the best baseball player that ever lived and don't ever forget that. I'm certain Uncle Sam watches all the games from Baseball Heaven. When I join him in that heavenly world, the first question he'll ask is, "Whatever happened to love at the old ball game?"

My friend Ida also had one love – baseball. In those days, tickets were affordable for nearly everyone so whenever possible, she was at Fenway Park rooting for her team, the Boston Red Sox and her favorite players, Walter Dropo and Teddy Williams. They were among the top players of their time and to this day, some of the records Williams set still stand unbroken. He never made over thirty thousand dollars a year even in his best record setting years, but he did it for love of the game. And Dropo and Williams never charged for an autograph. Dropo became the catalyst for fulfilling my promise to Ida, the newspaper lady on Dover Street. On her next birthday, she told me she had tickets for the game at Fenway Park. I found out and contacted Walter Dropo and told him Ida's story, and that she was going to be at the game that day. He arranged a surprise for her with Ted Williams. Before the game, Walter and Ted came out of the dugout and surprised her with birthday wishes, autographed baseballs, and dedicated that day's game to her. For Ida, it was a day to remember

for the rest of her life, and I was happy to have made good

on my promise to do something nice for her someday.

Chapter 16
New York New York

We had been at the Bradford three months and closed in December of 1947 when Sally said, "Shadow, we have been booked in New York." I jumped up and down and screamed for joy.

"New York," I yelled, "New York. You mean we are going to New York? Really?"

"Yes," she laughed, "The Sally Keith Revue has been booked into The Greenwich Village Inn in New York City. Secretary, get on the phone and call Walter Winchell. Get us some advance publicity. Your job is cut out for you. In the meantime I am going to make arrangements for you and

Sharples and Naples to work a few spots on the way up. That will cover your salary for a few weeks while Murph, Pepper and I head down to New York and put together a band, hire chorus girls and a boy singer."

"Why do I have to do that," I asked?

"Okay Secretary, here's another lesson. When we get booked, Paul Jordan, our agent, gets us money for the performance plus traveling expenses, but only one way. So what I have to do is work bookings so we get traveling expenses paid all the way up and all the way back. I have a circuit booked for us all the way to Montreal and back. We will be in New York City until spring then we will head up to the Finger Lakes in Geneva for the summer. In September we head back to Boston by way of Connecticut."

"I see."

"And as for you, Pepper is choreographing a new feature number for you. You will now be Statue, the Girl in Gold. Murph is working on a drum arrangement and your body will be nude except for a G-string and gold pasties. You will be completely covered in gold paint, except for your face, which will be covered by a mask. We are working on shower arrangements now because you can't be painted for more than 30 minutes. We have to get you on and off. But it's a great gimmick and no one that I know is doing it right now. So get in there with Pepper and Murph and start learning the steps, Statue."

Murph Rubinstein was on the drums pounding out the beat. His wife Pepper Russell had the recording of *Desert Caravan* on the phonograph. She placed a gold mask on my face, and while facing me, she raised her arms over her head had me follow every move she made in precision.

Soon I was behaving like a statue of gold with no expression, stiff like a chunk of gold. Within a few hours, I was no longer Shadow. I was Statue.

I had written a release and sent it to Walter Winchell as Sally had requested, and in a few days, I was packed and ready to go. I had my train tickets to New York with a stop in a club just out of New York City where Sharples and Naples and I would perform. I was the feature attraction, they the comedy stars. We would do "The Politician" and "Madam Kazaza" to keep them polished for our New York opening. A boy singer would be brought in to sing for my parade number. It sounded easy, but I had never been away from home. I had to leave Granny and Princess and all my friends to go to the big city of New York alone. Although I had been to New York many times with my mother to see shows and meet show people, I had never been that far alone. I had never even been to summer camp. One time when I was about ten years old, Granny paid for two weeks for me at a camp in the White Mountains, but when she turned around to leave me there, I kicked and screamed and cried until she took me by the hand and put me back on the train with her back to Boston. The camp counselor said that I should be tied to a post and horsewhipped. Granny said, "I am glad I didn't leave you there with that counselor's attitude."

So there I was packing to leave town with a revue. I felt safe with Charlie Naples and Wally Sharples, and the train ride was comfortable. We practiced lines, had lunch in the dining car, and when we arrived at our destination, the owners had a car waiting to drive us to the club. There was only one dressing room back stage, and a chorus of four girls and me sharing it, so Sharples and Naples said they would set up a little spot in the wings and let us have our privacy. That plan went out the window when a buxom blonde woman in a bright blue dress popped in leading a handsome young man and informed us that this was his dressing room, and we would have to give him space. We all looked a little puzzled by the audacity of the request. How could this woman expect five girls to give up their dressing room to a boy singer? When we got a good look at him we discovered he was very young and very handsome with big blue eyes and almost black hair. I hope he sings as good as he looks I thought. After all, he would be singing "A Pretty Girl is Like a Melody" for my parade number. She proceeded to separate the dressing room down the middle by stringing a rope across the room and hanging a sheet from it.

We looked at each other with open mouths. "Is this lady for real? Who is she? Who is this guy? And she's old enough to be his mother!"

"She must be his angel. You know the one who pays to have his teeth capped, his singing lessons and such while he is in New York waiting for a big break."

That was news to me. I had never heard of that kind of angel.

"What is his name?" I asked the woman.

"His name is Robert," she answered curtly, "Robert Goulet. And he does not wish to be annoyed by a bunch of silly chorus girls."

Who does this old woman think she is, we thought? Who wants that dumb kid anyhow? We have rich Stage Door Johnny's begging for our company. Not one of us would waste time on an unknown boy singer no matter how cute he was. We'd get even with her for her arrogance and insults. She combed his hair, applied his make-up, buttoned his shirt and tied his bow tie. While she prepared him for his show, we were preparing as well. When she finished, she stepped out to get him the glass of water he'd requested, and we went to work.

We pulled back the sheet, turned our backs to him, and in unison like a well-rehearsed chorus, we pulled down our net pants and flashed him five of the prettiest bottoms he had undoubtedly ever seen. They were no comparison to that fat, chunky, bleached blonde courtesan of his. Robert Goulet gasped, then laughed like a child who had just seen Santa Claus. We put the sheet back, pulled up our net pants, and when the old woman returned, life went on backstage as usual.

The show was a big hit – standing room only every night for two weeks. The sketches were hilarious, Sharples and Naples were a comedic talent, and my Hawaiian number stopped the show every night, especially when I twirled the flowers on my bra. When Robert Goulet crooned "A Pretty Girl is Like a Melody" for me, I had never paraded to more melodic tones.

Chapter 17
Greenwich Village Inn

We boarded a train for the trip into New York City. The taxi trip from Grand Central Station to the hotel was like a grand procession through a great kingdom – down Broadway, through Times Square, lights everywhere, store fronts full of merchandise – it felt like a dream and I felt like Cinderella in her coach approaching the castle. Only my castle was a hotel across from Madison Square Garden. I learned one thing about New York taxi drivers. They are full of conversation and keep you entertained, but be prepared to carry your own luggage.

In the hotel elevator, a young handsome gentleman introduced himself. "Hello. My name is Willie Pepp, and may I know yours?"

"Lily Ann Rose," I smiled, "I am the feature attraction at the Greenwich Village Inn. We open tomorrow night. Maybe you'll come to see the show."

When the elevator stopped, the operator opened the door for me, and as I stepped out he whispered, "Willie Pepp is the welter-weight boxing champion of the world."

I smiled back at Willie, but the title meant nothing to me.

"I'll be seeing you soon," he said and the doors closed.

My bags were already in the room so I went straight to Sally's room to get the rundown on the show.

"Statue," she began, "we have our work cut out for us. The piece you wrote for Walter Winchell worked. He gave us a few lines in his column, and we're sold out for opening night. Keep writing those good advances and start working on some reviews. You might do some advances for when we go upstate too."

"I can do that. What time is rehearsal? I want to call Granny and tell her I got to New York City all right. I sure miss her cooking. I'd give anything for a good Sicilian dinner right now. A dish of her pasta with clam sauce is just what I need."

"Statue," Sally said, "this town is full of good food. After rehearsal tonight we'll go try some of it at Leon and Eddies then we'll head out for the Stork Club. There is a young singer and a comic playing there that I want to catch. I think their names are Martin and Lewis. I'm looking for an act to take up to Lake Geneva with us. I'm thinking maybe a talent show. In the meantime let's get moving. Tonight's the last free night we have before our opening."

When I walked into the Greenwich Village Inn for rehearsal and saw my life size poster in the lobby, I felt like I was walking into a performers heaven. The stage was semi-circular and high off the shiny marble dance floor. The band was on stage rehearsing and the sound was symphonic. The tables were set and all had reserved signs on them.

Gary Marshall was the young male singer that Sally had booked for the show. When we rehearsed "A Pretty Girl is Like a Melody" it was like he was imitating Tony Martin. Then he began to sing "Softly, as in a Morning Sunrise" and when he finished he said, "I'd better record that before Martin does." This had been Martin's big hit, so I didn't think that was one bit funny.

Bobby English, the emcee interrupted us and introduced himself. "Forgive me, but I think you need a better parade number than that "Pretty Girl" thing. It's trite. Every showgirl in the business has used it. Let's do something different this time. I know an old song from the twenty's it goes like this: 'A little bit independent.' I'll sing it for you if you like," he said.

"I like," I said, "but we have to ask Sally. She is the boss."

English did the number for Sally and she loved it. "It's in," she cried.

Bob Dorian, a movie star that Sally had booked for the show, had played a convict in a lot of dark crime movies with Jimmy Cagney. A real bad guy. He turned out to be the sweetest guy I'd met in a long time. We became very good friends and spent a lot of time together. I was a real fan of his act in which he did a monologue called "The Last Mile" as a soprano sang in the background. It was based on an old Cagney movie about a prisoner on death row about to walk to the electric chair. The act was very classy and polished.

The chorus girls Pepper had selected were beautiful and good dancers. I especially liked Connie, an Italian girl from Brooklyn. She took me under her wing and taught me a lot about New York and life in show business. On Sunday, she invited me to her home and I got hopelessly lost on the subway to Brooklyn. When I finally found her place, I enjoyed a real New York home-cooked Italian dinner. It helped ease my longing for Boston and Granny's great cooking.

After rehearsal that night, we went to Leon and Eddies nightclub then to the Twenty One Club to see Martin and Lewis as Sally promised, but to our dismay, we were not allowed admission no matter how much Sally argued. Unescorted women were not allowed into the showroom, so we didn't get to see the new comedy rage team. But I sent a scathing item about it to Walter Winchell for Sally the next day and Winchell printed it.

On opening night, the show was a big hit and we got standing ovations after every act. I received a note from Willie Pepp to join him at his table between shows. Sally was happy to let me go sit with the "Welter Weight Champion of the World," but she warned me, "Eat but don't drink. I want you to stay sober, besides, you're underage." Sally got a percentage of every dime the club took in including food and drinks. The food on the menu was expensive and the service was extremely slow. I later discovered that the reason for the slow service. There was no kitchen in the Greenwich Village Inn. When one placed an order, the waiter took it to a little restaurant next door. They prepared it to go and the waiter spread it out fancy for his customers in the Inn.

After the show, I joined Willie who introduced me to a gentleman seated with him. "Lily Ann, this gentleman is a television producer."

"Yes," he said, "I'm casting a show, which will be televised in six weeks. Have you ever seen the movie *Champion*?" "Yes, of course," I answered..

"We're doing a version of the movie which is being adapted by Rod Serling for Climax! Chrysler Theatre, and Willie thinks you're perfect for the Marilyn Maxwell part. We've been watching you perform for several days and agree with him. Come try out for that role? What do you say?"

"I'm stunned. I don't know what to say except I have to ask Sally. She's the boss."

"You'd have to stay in New York for rehearsal for a few months until broadcast date. Of course, you'll get union scale – one-hundred-seventy-five dollars for the show and two rehearsals at fifty dollars each."

"Gee, that's not very much. I make one-hundred-seventy-five a week plus expenses right now. That means I'd have to live for weeks in New York without pay. I don't know. I'll have to think about it. Gosh imagine me on television. Who would I be working with?"

"Oh, just some unknowns like yourself. Jack Palance and some guy named Clint Eastwood. I'm sure you've never heard of them. We'll be back tomorrow night, and you can give me your answer then."

Willie said, "Lily Ann, this is your chance. Take it!

I rushed back to the dressing room and told Connie the chorus girl. She said, "For God's sake, Lily Ann do it. Don't turn this down."

"But if I leave the show, how will I live for months in New York without pay?"

"I'll take you to the agency where we go. We model for photographs for True Detective Magazine and get paid twenty-five bucks for every picture they use. With your body, you'd make a fortune."

I caught Sally in her dressing room and told her about the offer.

Sally threw up her hands. "Statue, are you nuts. No, of course you'll not take the silly offer. You make that much now plus you get to wear my diamond necklaces, white fox fur, and drive my gold Cadillac. Why on earth would you give that up?"

"Well, it is a chance to be on television," I answered. That was the only advantage I could think of.

"Statue, use your brain. Forget Willie Pepp, Studio One, and television. Television will never amount to anything."

Chapter 18
Totie Fields

After five months at the Greenwich Village Inn, we boarded the train for Lake Geneva. The train wound it's way upstate to the finger lake country through some of the most scenic places on earth. Those of us who related New York to skyscrapers and museums, Broadway and bright lights, subways and taxicabs, were overwhelmed with the natural beauty outside the window. To us, the mountains, forests, lakes and green expanse just a few miles from the noisy excitement of Manhattan, was a geographic wonder. The glorius countryside eased my loneliness for the moment.

On that train ride away from the world I had lived in for 17 years, I had time to contemplate my new-found self. I'd been in love with love since I could remember, but Frank had pummeled that desire nearly to death. I vowed to withhold my natural tendencies to love and never again leave myself open to such brutality. I would reserve my need to love for those who couldn't hurt me. I was trying hard to find the happy, carefree teenager I was before that life-changing opening night last year and the unaccustomed beauty of the area prompted me to write a poem:

Do you know Lily Ann Rose?

The blue-eyed girl

Whose innocence shows

The naive young girl

With the Roman nose

Where can I find Lily Ann Rose?

When the train arrived at the lodge, we were taken to our lodgings on Lake Geneva. We scarcely had time to place our personal belongings in our cabins then it was off to Club Geneva to unpack wardrobe, meet the band, rehearse, and get the show ready to open. Sally had hired a husband and wife comedy team from Boston to join the show in Geneva. Georgie Johnston and Totie Fields were two of the sweetest people I had ever met and a joy to work with. Georgie worked as Master of Ceremony's and Totie did a hilarious stand up comedy routine. She was four-foot-nine in high heels and pudgy and used her short, fat, body as the butt of her jokes. She slew the audience when she did her one-liners about her little Jewish fingers and feet.

Totie made up jokes about me which did not demean me. The one I remember best is, "I have come to know Lily Ann Rose really well, and contrary to what you may think, she is a real homebody." The audience would laugh like, yeah sure! Totie who was a master of comedic timing would pause a moment then add, "Yes, there should be a body like hers in every home!" The audience would howl. The weeks I spent working on Lake Geneva with Georgie Johnston and Totie Fields were some of the happiest of my short stardom. Eventually Georgie gave up his career to manage Totie. She became a comedy star and a favorite on Ed Sullivan's Show and a frequent guest on Merv Griffin's and Dinah Shore's talk shows until she died of diabetes complications at age forty-eight. Totie Fields will always hold a special place in my heart as a special human being and my favorite female comedian.

Chapter 19
Summer of Blossoming

This summer, my life could well be paralleled with the Finger Lakes of New York in just a few words, deep, dark, and containing hidden passages. But, as the summer blossomed, so did I. Lake Geneva was a beautiful body of water – deep blue in color, surrounded by a green shoreline, and quiet, except for the occasional roar of an outboard motor spewing white foam in its wake.

Sal, the young trumpet player in the band, picked me up nearly everyday in his hand crafted mahogany speedboat, and as we sped around the lake, we talked of family and dreams. Sal was attending college in Syracuse and came from an Italian family similar to mine. Whenever he had the chance, he pushed the hope of me returning home and back to school. He was getting to me, and thoughts of home and Granny plagued me night and day. But when I remembered the hard work and sacrifice it took to become the star I had dreamed of becoming, I was torn. I was working now, fulfilling that dream. What more could I want? Love, had been at the top of my list, but Frank had soured that dream. I came close to confiding in Sal as the boat cut into the crests of water on Lake Geneva, but my heart remained closed. Still, I was homesick and lonesome.

"Sal," I shouted one day over the roar of the engine, "I know what I have to do to relieve this darkness in me. Take me back to the cabin. I have to talk to Sally while I have the courage."

As the boat sped back to the dock, the urge to go home for a visit with Granny and her Italian pasta became overwhelming. The boat had barely bumped into the dock when I jumped out and hurried to Sally's cabin. She was sleeping, but I pounded on the door until she woke up.

"Sally, I really need some time off. I need to go home for a while – to Granny and her home-cooking. I promise I'll come back. All I am asking for is a week off. Please? Please? Please?'

"Secretary." She never stopped calling me by her pet names. "The show is doing too well, and we're under contract. You must learn to honor your commitments or the top agents will label you undesirable. You're just beginning a career, and running back to your Granny is not good for your image."

"But, I miss her so much. It's been six months since I've been home."

Sally thought a minute, "Okay, tell you what I'll do. I'll pay her fare to come up here by Pullman for a week and stay with you. She'll be my guest and will have a seat at a front table for dinner every night. How does that sound?"

"Oh Sally, thank you, thank you. I'll call her right away. Thank you, thank you, thank you," I yelled all the way out the door and headed directly to the front desk to call Granny.

The week she stayed with us at Lake Geneva was the most outstanding week of my life. Having her in the audience applauding loudly every night, gave the entire show an enormous boost – the show improved with her spirit. Not only was Granny what we all needed, her visit made my summer bearable, and I was so proud to have her in the audience. I usually got a standing ovation for my finale, and every night when I came out to join Granny at her table she had tears in her eyes.

"Why are you crying, Granny?" I asked the first night.

"You work so hard and you dance so beautifully, it just sends shivers through me," she answered..

I didn't ask her any more. I just took it as a tribute to my work. After all, she had been watching stage shows since the 1920's, and if I was good enough to inspire her to tears, I had to accept it as the greatest compliment I could ever want. She became my biggest fan after that and later, in collaboration with Aunt Lillian, and Margie, put together a scrapbook about Lily Ann Rose.

Life on the road was much more bearable for me after that, and thoughts of going back to Boston and school was pushed further back in my head. Sal still tried to convince me that going back to school was the answer, but it was not in the cards for this fifteen year-old star chaser.

We had six more weeks on the contract to fulfill. Summer was fading away into fall and soon Labor Day, our last weekend, would be here. This vacation spot on Lake Geneva in New York's Finger Lake Region would be covered in snow and sealed up for the winter.

Before Granny left for Boston and home, she filled me in on all the news. Carol, my friend with the lovely closet, had asked to move in with her and Granny let her have my room. When as a teenager, Carol lost all her family to tuberculosis she needed more comforting and love than she got from her aunt. Granny was there for her. I was grateful for the chance to help the friend who had loaned me her best dress for my big audition with Sally Keith.

Also as luck would have it, another friend, Johnny Goverman whose father owned the drug store on Dover Street, came to visit Granny and met Carol. They fell in love and were now engaged to be married as soon as Johnny graduated from College. So the summer had been good all around for Granny, Carol and me.

Chapter 20
Montreal

Sally was making plans for the winter. "Secretary," she said, "remember what I told you about expenses? They're paid one way coming out but not going back, so I've booked in a circuit that will get us back to Boston. You'll have a starring position at the Gayety Burlesque Theater in Montreal. From there you go to Chicago, then back to New York, Connecticut, Rhode Island and Massachusetts. You'll be home by Christmas. How does that sound?"

Home by Christmas. Home by Christmas. Those words sent music through my brain. "Oh yes, yes." I jumped up and down. "When do I leave?"

"Get on the phone with our agent, Paul Jordan, in Boston. He'll set up the itinerary. Then come back and we'll select your costumes, music and numbers. I think the Hawaiian number is one of your best. Also the one you do with 'A Little Bit Independent in Your Walk.'" Sally thought for a minute and said, "Say I have another idea. Can you write a parody to 'I'm a Big Girl Now?'"

I got right to work on it and came up with this parody:

> I'm a big girl now
>
> I wanted to be treated like a big girl now
>
> I used to want to be a perfect thirty-eight
>
> But now I drive an Oldsmobile Eighty-eight
>
> I'm a big girl now

We worked it up into an intro, and Sally wrapped me in her white fox fur and added a few diamonds and pearls. She had Murph arrange the music. I talked the words with the music. We had an opening number that no other stripper was doing. Sally was very conscientious about being original and not copying other performers.

So after Labor Day, I packed up my costumes and the beautiful wardrobe I had accumulated. I was most fascinated with the net bras and panties I had custom made for me by a New York costumer. They were flesh colored, shear, very shear, with ruffles on the rear end. I thought the ruffles covered the butt pretty well, and I couldn't wait to show them off. I practiced shaking those ruffles until I was a combination of Sally Rand, Sally Keith, and Peaches only, I thought, more so. I could stand still and make those ruffles move like lightening bugs in a jar. We had worked out music to "As the Saints go Marching In" for this number and what a finale. When we tried it out in Lake Geneva it stopped the show every night. Sally was ecstatic. We had a winner. She was proud to book me as her protégée in a star billing.

I kissed Sally goodbye and took the train to Montreal full of hope for the future. I was finally the star of the show. The Gayety was a lovely theater in the heart of the theater district. After the first show, I went next door to the Stage Door Restaurant for a between shows dinner. I was alone at a table when the waiter approached me and yelled at me in French. I didn't understand a word he was saying, and I told him so, in English. But he apparently didn't understand a word I said and it turned into a screaming match with him yelling something in French and me yelling "I don't understand" in English. We were getting no where until a man approached the table. He carried a walking stick and was dressed in white shirt, a tie, and a vest that a king would be comfortable wearing. With his gray hair neatly combed, he looked like royalty.

"Pardon me, Mademoiselle, may I help you?" He spoke with a deep French accent but perfect English.

"Yes" I answered. "This waiter is screaming at me, and as far as I know, I've done nothing. I can't understand a word he's saying. Can you get him to stop?"

"Pardon, Mademoiselle. He is simply asking you to move from this table."

"But why? I only have a short time between shows, and I'd like to eat my supper and leave. I don't wish to move. I want service."

"But Mademoiselle, I know you are the star of the show next door, and we wish to serve you, but this section is reserved."

"Reserved, for who?" I asked.

"It is hard for me to say this to such a charming and obviously young lady, but how do I say, this section is reserved for, you know . . .?"

"No I don't know. What are you talking about?"

He searched for the words and finally, he got it out. "Dear Mademoiselle, this section is reserved for... for... certain ladies-of-the-evening"

"You mean prostitutes?" I was horrified.

"Yes, Mademoiselle, yes."

"Oh my! I'm so embarrassed. Of course I'll move."

"My name is Pierre La Simone. Will you be so kind to join me at my table for dinner?"

He put out his arm. I took it and he escorted me out of the ladies-of-the-evening section to his private table. He told me he was a member of the Canadian Parliament and his dear friend who owned this restaurant, was ill. He was in charge of it in the meantime. He said he had seen my show and knew exactly who I was. He asked if he could show me about Montreal while I was in town.

"Yes," I answered. "I'd love to see Montreal." After all, I hadn't been out of Boston but once or twice in my life. "But, I have a show to do every day and I must be at the theater by 2:00 in the afternoon,"I informed him.

"That is no problem. I will pick you up tomorrow morning at say10:00?"

"I'll be ready but I must hurry back for the evening performance. Thank you again for your courtesy. I promise I'll not sit in that section again during my stay in Montreal."

"If you don't mind, I will be your personal escort for your entire stay. Oui?"

"Yes, if you promise to give me a lesson in French."

"Oui, Mademoiselle. Until tomorrow. I will pick you up in the lobby."

The hotel was located conveniently next door to the theater. I was up bright and early and in the lobby at 10:00. There was Pierre and outside was a long black limousine. Wow, I had never seen anything so classy since Jack Kennedy's and at funerals. The chauffeur opened the door for me and I entered a new world. Pierre sang a lovely song to me in the car. It was called "Le Mer." I had never heard it before, and it became one of my favorites.

Pierre picked me up every morning at 10:00 a.m. and we toured all the Montreal sights including the wonderful cathedral on the hill that all the tourists love to visit. He always had me back in time for show time and took me to dinner every night. And I did learn some French – Oui, La, comment allez vous, Monsieur, Madame, sil vous plait.

On the day I left Montreal, I received a note of thanks from Pierre. In it, he thanked me for all the lovely moments I had given him, and he was grateful I had made him feel young again. In the box that accompanied the note was a recording of "Le Mer", which I treasured and played for many years. To this day when I hear that song, I think of Montreal and my dear friend in the Canadian Parliament.

Chapter 21
Barbara English AKA Babs London

The Watch and Ward Society and their censors never gave up their relentless quest for "morality," on the burlesque stages in Boston. Every stripper and exotic dancer was subject to arrest for the slightest allusion to sex. Lily Ann Rose was not alone in the banned in Boston category. So, it was not unusual for a stripper to change her name when playing a date in the Boston area. One of my favorite alias' was Lloma Rhodes. So when I walked into a club featuring one of my best friends from the chorus at the Casino Theater sharing the bill for Feature Attraction with me, I was delighted. Barbara English was billed as Babs

232

London. As I entered the showroom on my way to the dressing room I overheard a woman talking to her date.

"I know Barbara English and Babs London will never be as good as she is."

I wanted to tell her, "lady you don't know what you are talking about. Barbara English is Babs London." But under the circumstances, I chose to keep quiet. After all, we were both banned in Boston.

I had played Newport, Rhode Island often between dates and had built up quite a following of sailors. They were the best audience in the world and such a dancers delight to which to play. Handsome in their navy blue bell bottoms and crisp white caps, neat as a shiny painted deck of a Navy Destroyer, and not afraid to cheer, clap, and howl for the beauty of their choice on stage. A group had hitchhiked down to Massachusetts to see Lily Ann Rose perform.

I went on first that night and opened the show with one of my sexiest performances, at least I thought it was sexy. I got lots of howls and a few poundings on the floor and maybe two encores. I tried harder each time even tried to imitate Peaches and shake it to *Saints Go Marchin' In,* but I could not outdo Babs London, who of course was my friend from my Casino days, Barbara English.

Barbara came on stage and centered herself in front of the sailors in the front row and worked her heart out for them. Each time she moved they roared, louder and louder, and louder. They kept bringing her back, for encore after encore. She centered herself in front of them in the first row and over and over, they screamed and hollered for more. I loved Barbara, but I was beginning to get a little jealous. After all I thought, these sailors came all the way to see me,

Lily Ann Rose, and Barbara English is stealing my thunder. But I handled it well and did my best.

After the show Barbara and I rode home to Boston together and talked about the evening's success. I told her I was a little put out because the sailors came all the way from Newport to see me, and they screamed , hollered, and pounded, a lot louder for her than me.

Barbara looked at me with those deep sincere brown eyes and said, "Lily Ann, why do you think they were yelling louder for me than you. You don't think it's because I'm so much taller than you."

"I don't know, I can't figure it out. I tried so hard, too."

"Well kiddo, I will tell you my secret. I cut out the front of my net pants and I was flashing them bare pussy. That's why they were screaming louder for more.

I was mortified, "No," I said.

"Yes," she laughed.

"But why? Why did you do that.?" I was so sincere.

Barbara English answered with all the patriotism a lady could muster, "Why, Lily Ann Rose, those sailors are out there defending our country. That's the least I could do for those brave, handsome swabbies."

I will always remember Barbara English with love and fondness.

Chapter 22
April Starr

"Get that little cunt in here. Now! I want to talk to her."

April Starr was screaming. Her black eyes were on fire with rage. Her long raven black hair was flying along with her jealousy about her face. It was my first performance after leaving Montreal. I got the feeling that this was not going to be one of my favorite bookings.

"What is wrong with you April." Paul Jordan the booking agent, interrupted her to keep her from marching on stage. He had met my train in Hartford, Connecticut and accompanied me to the one-night club date as Sally had asked.

"What's wrong? She has the audience wild, that's what's wrong."

"So, what's wrong with getting the audience all stirred up for you?" Paul thought it was hilarious and good for his business.

"Just shut up you goddam ten-percenter. People like you are killing burlesque. Get her in here. NOW!"

"Calm down, April. I can't stop her in the middle of her number. And besides, you'll never get on stage. That audience will be yelling for her for twenty minutes."

I rushed off stage into the wings, breathless after performing my Hawaiian dance number as the opening act. It was exhilarating. I had wanted to do a good show but I had never expected this. The audience was pounding on the tables and the floor. I had stopped the show.

April Starr was waiting for me, her black eyes wide open. She tore into me. "Do you know who I am?" she screamed in my face.

"Yes, April Starr." I answered.

"No. I mean who I really am. I'm the star of this goddam show. That is who I am."

"I know that." I fooled around with the flowers on my bra, reminding her how they spun when I shook my shoulders. "I'm just the opening act, right?" I smoothed the grass skirt around my hips.

"Listen you little cunt, I don't know what you were doing out there, but you gotta be doing something outrageous. What have you got under that grass skirt? Come on, I want to see. What have you got, a hole cut in your underwear? Come on you must be showing something to make those Johnny's yell like that."

239

"Nothing. I am not showing anything. Teddy English said I had to show my fur cap, but I refuse to do that, so I shaved it." Teddy English was master of ceremonies.

"You what?" She was screaming so loud her face was turning bright red.

"I shaved it." I answered.

"Paul, did you hear that. She is flashing a bare pussy."

"I am not."

"You are too." She lunged at me and grabbed my hair but Paul pulled her off me.

Teddy fell on the floor laughing. He had teased me in the dressing room earlier about showing my little fur cap. I had believed him and before the show shaved my legs all the way up to my belly button.

"I wouldn't do such a naughty thing, but just in case I wanted to be prepared so I cleaned it up." I looked Teddy

English in the eye. "You did tell me I had to show my little fur cap, right?"

Teddy stopped laughing and looked at me, "Sorry kid, I was kidding. You don't have to show anything. Just go on out there and do your encore before the audience takes the curtain down. Paul and I will straighten her out."

Paul looked at April and said, "Just be nice and I'll let you open the show for the remainder of the run. Lily Ann Rose will close, and we'll all have our jobs. How does that sound?"

"Kiss my ass," she said, "I'm quitting."

"The audience was still hollering for more and bringing me back for encore after encore. "What am I supposed to do? I am the star of this goddam show," April Starr screamed at Paul.

"If I were you," said Paul Jordan "I'd take a dance lesson from her."

I stepped into the wings and Paul turned me around and sent me back out to an audience still screaming and pounding the floor for more. Despite April's outburst it remains one of the fondest memories of my career as a dancer. No matter how good a performance it is, it isn't often a dancer stops the show.

Chapter 23
Raymond Patriacca

The train ride to Providence, Rhode Island from Hartford wasn't a very long one, but there were too many stops, and I was tired of traveling. All I wanted at that point was to be home in Boston, but I had one week booking here and still had Chicago to do. When we finally pulled into the Providence station, I followed the conductor off, hailed a cab to take me to the Valley Club and was gone before the train pulled out.

At the club, the stage curtains were open and the band was waiting for me before beginning the rehearsal. They gave me the once over, comparing me to the last feature attraction, Sally Rand. It was obvious this club used only high-priced New York entertainers, not local girls who were banned in Boston. I took the music from my case and ran through the numbers with the band. I didn't shake a muscle or show them anything and they seemed disappointed. They were unable to pass judgement on this unknown.

When I got to my dressing room to unpack, I found that my watch was missing. The last time I had seen it was when I removed it to wash up in the train's bathroom. "Oh, no," I cried, "not my beautiful watch." That watch meant so much to me. It was a twelfth birthday gift from Blackie Alum's parents. Blackie was my best friend during the summers I spent with Margie. He had a sister, Rita, an Aunt Bebe, and wonderful parents who owned a coffee and donut shop on Dover Street. The Alum's were Syrian and their neighborhood was a mix of Syrians, Lebanese, and Greeks, with a few Italians and some newly arrived, displaced Europeans from other countries. The Alum's were kept busy running the shop, and Blackie and I were left alone a lot to listen to Frankie Laine records. Blackie was a big fan and had every Laine recording ever made.

Blackie's cousin Frank was around a lot and they got a big kick out of teasing me. One day when Blackie was home sick and Frank and I were keeping him company, they sent me into the kitchen to get Blackie a glass of water. Unbeknown to me, they had planted a dead mouse in the middle of the kitchen floor and planned to scare me with it. I brought the water to Blackie and the boys looked at me in astonishment! Why, hadn't I screamed? Frank and Blackie rushed into the kitchen, and lo and behold, the mouse was gone. "Are you sure you didn't see anything?" They asked over and over and I assured them I didn't know what they were talking about. So in the end they figured the scheming mouse must have played dead and outwitted them. We all had a good laugh.

Once or twice a week, Blackie and I were invited to supper at Aunt Bebe's for Kibbee, my favorite Syrian dish. No one ever came close to making Kibbee like Aunt Bebe. After dinner as we sat around the table drinking demitasse of Turkish coffee, Aunt Bebe would sing to us in her lovely soprano voice. My favorite song in her repertoire was "Are You Lonesome Tonight" with words she had written about a true incident. A woman named Ruth who was awaiting a death sentence for killing her husband.

Are you sorry tonight,

That you killed him that night

Does your heart fill with pain

When you think of Lorraine

Tell me Ruth, Are you sorry tonight.

Lorraine was Ruth's daughter.

Blackie's parents had given me that special watch and now it was gone. I was heartbroken and could think of nothing else. When show time was announced, I put on my stage persona, walked out on the stage and gave the best performance I had in me. That night I got a standing ovation and so many encores, I can't remember. When I finally got off-stage, I again moped about my lost watch.

While I was removing my costume, the door to my dressing room opened and the boss of the club stood there.

"A gentleman knocks before entering a ladies dressing room," I said.

"I own this place. I can do as I please."

"You can start," I said firmly, "by going out and knocking first."

"Okay, kid, I won't bother you again. Just get dressed, go out front, and sit at the ringside table. The big man wants you to sit with him, so hurry up."

"I'm sorry, but I don't drink and I do not sit on demand with customers. Just get out and give him my regrets."

"Look at us acting like we're a big star." He put his hand on his hip and stuck it out mockingly. If you know what's good for you, you'll get out there. But for the big man, Raymond Patriacca, you wouldn't even be here right now. We never use local girls – we don't waste our money on you. We get the big time strippers out of New York. The only reason you're here is he, personally, asked for Lily Ann Rose. So get out there, and fast."

He left and slammed the door, huffing and mad as a stripper who'd just lost her G-string. I followed him arguing as we entered the big dining room. There were two sailors in uniform at the bar. I said to the bartender, "See those two sailors over there, give them anything they want to drink, and put it on my tab. They are my guests for the evening."

"You have no tab here! You have no job here! You are cancelled as of this moment!"

"Good," I said, "I'll be on my way to Boston as soon as I can pack."

Just then the gentleman, and I do stress gentleman, who had been sitting at the ringside table sauntered up. "Okay Vincenti, that's quite enough. I'll handle this myself."

He was tall and handsome in a beige suit and dark tie. His hair was salt and pepper gray, and he looked about my Grandmother's age – fiftyish.. He could have been the grandfather or the father I never had. I found out later he was Raymond Patriacca, the ruler of the northeast Mafia.

"Please Miss Rose, accept my apology for Vincenti's rude behavior. You are not cancelled and you are not obligated to drink or sit with anyone, not even me. Accept my apology and let's start over. He put out his hand to shake mine and I reached out, shook his, then I put my arms around him and kissed him in the Italian tradition – on each cheek. He was very moved by my reaction. I took his arm and walked with him to his table and sat proudly at Raymond Patriacca's table every night I was in the Valley Club. He was a wonderful listener. I told him of all my hopes and dreams and disappointments and cried about the precious Longene Whitenhauer watch I had lost on the train. I was held over for one more week, but I couldn't stay longer because of my Chicago booking.

On the night of my last appearance at the Valley Club, I answered a knock at my dressing room door. Vincenti stood with a gift wrapped box with an orchid on top which he handed to me. The note attached read, "To Lily Ann Rose. Thank you for a most memorable two weeks. Good luck in your career and I hope we meet again soon. Sincerely, Raymond Patriacca." When I opened the box, I cried out with joy for there it was a brand new shiny gold, Longene Whitenhauer watch.

Chapter 24

Chicago

It was October, 1949 when I arrived in Chicago and it felt dark – like the light of life was in hiding. Boston was cold, but in Chicago I was as colder than I had ever been. The wind blew across Lake Michigan like the hurricane of 1938 and the ice on the roads made the taxi slip and slide like a carnival ride. All I had to wear was the mink stole I used as a costume, but it sure felt good this day.

I hadn't heard from Sally for a while and felt that something was amiss between us. I hoped not and sent her a note when I got to Club 21 hoping to get a positive reply. There were two dressing rooms, one for the girls and one for the men and the other girls were already there when I arrived. The rooms were large with two rows of tables and long wall mirrors framed in electric light bulbs. The showgirls were from all over – Baby Rose from Canada, Bonnie Faye Adams from Detroit, Charmaine from Canada and Dawn Knight from good old South Boston are the ones I remember. Dawn and I became good friends immediately. It didn't take long before we realized this was not a place we wanted to be.

We weren't allowed out of the premises for meals between shows. We had to walk through a secret passage behind the bar to the back room of a greasy spoon next door. The chef/owner we nicknamed Monkey was very nice to us and took good care with our orders, but I could not eat the food. I would order, take one bite and leave the rest. Dawn, whose real name was Mary Ann Theresa Agnes

Crowe, decided I needed protecting and appointed herself my guardian. "Lily Ann didn't anyone ever teach you to eat everything on your plate?" she'd say.

"No, I said. "Granny never served anything she knew I wouldn't eat."

"Well it is about time you learned. From now on you will eat everything on your plate or you will sit there until you do."

Here I was in Chicago at the age of sixteen and being forced to clean my plate like a little child, but I did learn to eat the food. I was also learning more about life. As I stood in a line I thought was for the john, the girl in front of me passed me a smoking, smelly cigarette and said here take a drag. I took it between my fingers and put it up to my nose. "Ugh," I said, "it stinks." I passed it to the next girl in line.

When I told Dawn what happened and she told me it was dope. "It's good you passed on it. We have to get out of this place, fast. I haven't any money saved yet, but as soon as I do we're out of here."

Benny the bartender overheard us talking and whispered, "Hush, you two. Do you want to get hurt or worse, killed? The big guys aren't going to let you go. That's how this town is run. They tell you what you can do and what you can't. So if you want to live without getting cut up, do what I say. I like you two. You're younger than the others. I'll help but you must trust me. I'll let you know when it is safe to make a move. In the mean time just play along."

"Oh my gosh, Dawn," I said. "We really are captives in this awful place. Benny said they would cut us. Or worse, kill us. How'd you get here?"

"My agent booked me. He didn't tell me it'd be like this."

"Me too." I said. "I didn't think Paul would do this to me. Sally must be mad at me. At least we have each other."

Dawn and I walked back to the dressing room. The owner had given us our instructions, but until now, we didn't realize they were orders. We were not to date or leave with a customer, but were to sit at their tables, drink phony drinks – as many as we could and order twenty-five dollar bottles of champagne until their money was gone or they were thrown out. If the paying customer wanted sex, we would be replaced with a prostitute. We had to stay and work from 4 p.m. until 4 a.m. We were paid well for the phony drinks and champagne and our performances, but they gave us only enough of our money to live on and the rest they held back until they decided it was time for us to leave. This was not a life for Dawn nor me.

Every night we begged Benny to get us out of Chicago. He told us to be patient but to get our money out of the account buy purchasing anything of value that we could sell for cash. So we bought from the pitchmen who came in selling diamonds, watches, gold, furs, sequined dresses. The boss would sign the voucher and the bookkeeper would pay the pitchman for the purchase. I even bought a 1941 Buick and sold it back to the guy for half of what I paid for it. At least I had the cash and stashed it in my wardrobe trunk. For five months we did this. I had missed Christmas at home.

In the meantime, I sneaked out every night to see Sally Rand who was appearing at the club next door. She was the only positive memory I have of my stay in Chicago. Her feathers waved around her body so gracefully showing nothing but promising everything. They said to the awed audience that she was nude behind them. Her music was the most spellbinding I had ever heard a stripper use. It was my introduction to Claire De Lune. I knew those fans weighed a ton because when I had practiced a fan dance with Sally Keith while we were working on routines, I could barely lift one let alone swing it gracefully over my head and body – and Rand used not one fan, but two at a time. She was magnificent and I'm thrilled that I had the opportunity to see her. She was blonde and so tiny and dainty. The fans must have weighed almost as much as she did. And what a stage presence she had. For all the heartache I found in Chicago working for a mob boss with no heart, it was worth it to have known Sally Rand if just from a distance every night for nearly a week.

Then one evening, after five long months, Benny told us he was ready. He said to meet him at 9:00 the next morning at the club. We had pooled our money, hid it in my wardrobe trunk, and were to divide it 50-50 when we got home. That night we locked our trunks and called Railway Express to come and get them. They came for them the next morning. Benny helped us sneak our music and costumes out of the club. We packed them in our luggage and he drove us to the Greyhound Bus Terminal in Gary, Indiana. We were on our way home. In Buffalo, we were hit by a treacherous late spring snow storm. We stopped at a diner and the bus was not going anywhere until that storm passed. We ordered something to eat and after we'd paid the bill and tipped the waiter his fifteen cents, I said to Dawn, "We aren't broke yet. We have two nickels left," and held them up in the air. Dawn took one nickel from my hand and put it in the jukebox. I kept one for a telephone call. "Now we are truly broke." she said. We laughed, just very glad to be out of Chicago. Two young innocents from Boston who couldn't wait to get home. I called Paul Jordan, my agent, regarding my commitment to one more club date in Sudbury, Massachusetts just outside of Boston. Dawn vowed to quit the business and went home.

I arrived at my club date in Sudbury cold and tired from the Chicago bus trip. I decided I would wear my ruffled flesh-colored nets and really show off tonight. This was my last club date on the road, and I was going to give it my all. On stage that night, I put all the energy I had into my act. I got down to my net bra and shear ruffled net panties and shook like I had never shook before. The audience was screaming and pounding on the floor to the beat of "When the Saints Go Marching In." The drums were drumming and the trumpets blaring and the music and I were the only things on earth – that is until someone grabbed my wrist.

"Stop it. What are you doing?" I was forced to stop the dance and the music came to a dead still. A strange man had come onto the stage and grabbed me. "Somebody help me." I yelled, but that only made him tighten his grip so I couldn't move and it became painful.

When the boss came running onto the stage, the grabber held up a badge and said, "Keep away. I'm Trooper Manchester, and I'm placing this girl under arrest."

"No, no," I cried. "Let me go."

"I'm charging her with lewd and lascivious conduct. She's under arrest, and if any one tries to stop me he'll be arrested as an accessory. Now let us pass." He took me directly from the stage to the police car. It was the middle of March and I had no coat. I was shivering badly when we got to the town jail. Manchester shoved me into a chair at the desk sergeant's desk who began to throw questions at me.

"What's your full name?"

"Lily Ann Rose."

"How old are you?"

"Seventeen."

"Yeah sure. Seventeen. Come on you're at least 24."

"No, I'm really, seventeen. Born January 23, 1933."

"Have you ever been arrested before?"

"No."

The questions went on and on and after he was through, he told the photographer who was standing by, to get my picture. I was made to stand under bright lights while he had a good time for at least two hours taking my pictures, putting me into pose after pose. I felt that I was posing for

Life Magazine not mug shots for an arrest. I was in dire misery by the time that was finished, and Manchester ordered the Sergeant to lock me up. "The judge won't be in until Monday," he said to me, "so you'd better just get settled in." The sergeant took hold of my arm and shoved me into a cell.

"I want to call someone. Let me call my mother or my aunt." I screamed and cried for hours to no avail. I climbed up to the barred window and screamed to be let out. The next morning, a psychiatrist came into my cell. He was sent to talk to me because I couldn't stop crying.

I don't need a doctor. I need to go home." I said.

He was there to calm me down, but I would not be quiet. Never was I given a chance to make a phone call nor was I offered even the simple gesture of a set of warm clothes. On Sunday, after thirty-six hours, a matron brought me my suitcase which contained mainly costumes and evening dresses that were only somewhat warmer than the costume I was wearing. But thank heavens, the owner of the club in which I was arrested called my agent, Paul Jordan, who called Sally Keith who notified my family and found an attorney.

On Monday morning after sixty hours in detention when I was brought before a judge, Aunt Lillian had brought a Lord and Taylor black wool suit that Carol had lent for me to wear to court. The judge set a date for trial, and I was released on bail. Aunt Lillian, who had never missed a day of work in her life, went back to work in Charlestown and I took a taxicab home.

The ride home from Boston's South Station to 181 Shawmut Avenue gave me time to mull over the events of the past year. Gone were the carefree days when I had tagged along with Frank in his blue policeman's uniform. That happy day in June of 1947, when I had strode down Hanover Street dreaming of stardom seemed a lifetime away. Today I was coming home, not a star, but a notorious stripper, banned in Boston and awaiting trial for lewd and lascivious conduct, my dreams shattered.. As I struggled up the five flights of dark stairs with my heavy baggage, I entered an empty flat, tired and afraid for the future – fearful of going to jail. Sixty hours locked up in a cell was the worst feeling I had ever known, and I swore I would never again do anything that would get me arrested. I set my bags on Granny's kitchen floor, dropped my weary body onto my usual chair at her welcome table and knew that home had never looked so good. Here I would stay, await my court date, and pray for leniency.

Several days later, Granny was out shopping and the flat was cold and empty. I hadn't even walked out the front door since the day of my hearing when the phone rang. It was Frank.

"Lily Ann, I have to see you." he demanded, "I've got to speak to you, now."

"Frank, what more do you want from me? You raped me and now you demand I see you. How dare you?"

"I'm coming up now. Please, let me in and listen to what I have to say. I won't touch you. I promise."

I sat in the darkened kitchen and waited, remembering the times Frank sat at this same table with Granny and me, a cup of coffee in his hand. He stopped by nearly every morning before walking his beat and again after his shift. I couldn't help feeling sad when I thought about the love I had felt for him.

"Come in," I whispered when he appeared in the doorway. I was afraid to move.

"You look beautiful as always," he said.. "I was afraid the fast life of burlesque would stain you."

"Stain me." I was indignant. "After what you did to me what more could stain me?"

"What I did was your fault. You chased me. Remember how you held my hand as I walked the beat, telling me over and over, I love you Frank. Remember?"

"I remember I loved you, but my love was that of a sister or a daughter. I remember you took me to my first circus at Boston Garden. I remember every evening I sat on the stoop waiting for you to come on duty so I could walk the beat with you. I remember how much I loved you, six feet tall in your blue uniform. I remember times when I was little; you'd pick me up and let me pull the box for you. Yes, how well I remember." I paused a moment. "I also remember what you did to me that night in Soupy's apartment. What you stole from me. I remember how I dyed my hair black to match my insides, and the time I put my head in the oven nearly ending it all. I remember that you changed my life with your cruelty."

"Cruelty! You asked for it."

"What I was asking for was comfort and understanding, not rape. If that's what you wanted to say to me, get out of here before Granny comes home."

"Sit down a minute," Frank pleaded. "I have something else to tell you. Please.".

He seemed pale and drawn, not himself so I sat down and folded my hands in my lap. He reached for my hand. I pulled it back, terrified. My heart pounded. The front door was open, and I was ready to flee.

"I want you to hear this from me. I was struggling with a drunk over on Dover Street, trying to get him into the Paddy Wagon a few months ago, and he bit my wrist. I hit him with my billy club, and when I took him to the hospital, the doctor asked me to take off my jacket and shirt so he could treat my bite. He looked me over and told me he was more interested in an old mole on my arm than my bitten wrist. I hadn't noticed it had turned black. To make a long story short. It was cancer. They operated and removed it, but it had spread. The doctor said it was melanoma. I don't have much more time to live, and I just want to say goodbye – to tell you how much you've always meant to me."

"I meant what to you? You say it is my fault you raped me. You're not sorry! Just, I chased you! That's what you want me to admit so you die with a clear conscience?"

"Hey kid, don't make this hard on yourself. You asked for it. And again, I say you weren't a virgin."

"I'm sorry you're dying, Frank. But I won't help pull your soul from purgatory. Just say goodbye and leave me alone."

Frank rose from the chair, his eyes down, pale and frail. "Goodbye, Lily Ann," he said.

"Goodbye, Frank," I whispered as he walked out the door.

I felt an enormous weight rise from my heart. Confronting Frank had helped free me from the dark memory of that morning in Soupy's apartment. Free of the humiliation and shame and no more would I contemplate suicide. From this day on I would hold my head high. It was a joy to be in love with love once again.

Frank Gates died from melanoma cancer three months later.

Chapter 25

Finale

Friends and family rallied around me and called me in the days preceding the trial, which was set for May 15, 1950, offering to help in any way. Even my teacher, Miss Griswold, came to Granny's to give me courage. Ralph Sisson, who's mother owned the Liquor Store on Dover Street, offered to loan me his brand new car to drive up for the court date. I would have accepted, but I was still not licensed to drive. Sally had called me at Granny's after I got home and said she was sorry for what had happened to me. She offered her car also, but she couldn't drive us. Aunt

Lillian hired an attorney who offered to drive so that problem was solved.

Before trial day, Aunt Lillian marched me to Captain DiSassa's, office at Police Headquarters in Boston. She felt comfortable doing this because he was Uncle Pat's cousin. She sat me down in his office and said, "Tell him why you were arrested, Lily Ann."

"Yes, why were you arrested Lily?" he asked.

"The officer said I was lewd and lascivious."

"Were you?" he asked.

"I didn't think what I did was wrong. I was just doing my job. I didn't know it was lewd and lascivious. I don't even know what lewd and lascivious means."

"Lewd and lascivious means indecent."

"I thought I was just doing a good job."

"Your Aunt told me she didn't want you to have a job shaking your you-know-what in front of an audience. What are we going to do about that?"

"I don't know, honest. Being a star is all I have ever wanted – ever dreamed about. Ever since I saw Ann Corio and Bud Abbott and Lou Costello and Margie and Aunt Karin on stage, it's all I've ever wanted."

"Lily, there is a whole life for you out there. Your Aunt tells me you are very talented. Surely if you went back to school there is something you could succeed in."

"I don't know. Being a star is all I have ever wanted." I was crying.

Aunt Lillian put her arms around me. "Lily Ann, please don't cry. It's very important for you to listen to Captain DiSassa. He's trying to help you."

The Captain leaned forward. "I can only help you if you promise me and your Aunt that you will never step on stage again. Even so, I can't promise that I can get you out of this jam. You've broken the law and lawbreakers must pay the penalty. Mae West went to jail for thirty days for just showing her ankles. You did a lot more. Do you understand?"

"Yes. Please don't let them send me back. I promise I'll never break another law as long as I live."

"Look your Aunt in the eye and say, I promise."

Aunt Lillian held me and told me she loved me. I looked her in the eye and said, I promise I will never break the law again."

Captain DiSassa said, "Good. I can't promise anything, but I will make a phone call and put in a good word for you. Remember your promise. No more of this.

When Aunt Lillian and I walked out of his office, I was ready for my trial. Heartbroken, but ready. I really didn't want to give up my life on the stage, but I knew I had to. Aunt Lillian and I arrived at the courthouse early with my attorney. The courtroom was packed and people were milling about on the street and in the halls. They had come to see the infamous Lily Ann Rose who was banned in Boston. As for me, I just wanted to get it finished. Today, I was shaking, not to any drumbeat, but from pure fright at the possibility of being sentenced to a jail term. The hideous sixty hours in that cell were utmost in my thoughts. The promise I made to Aunt Lillian was one I would keep for the rest of my life.

"All rise." The judge entered the courtroom. In the expectant hush, I caught sight of the man who had grabbed my arm on the stage – Trooper Manchester in uniform this time.

The Court Officer read from the log. "The State of Massachusetts versus Lily Ann Rose on the charge of Lewd and Lascivious Conduct."

The Judge looked at me and said, "How do you plead?"

My attorney answered, "My client pleads not guilty, Your Honor."

Judge: "Call your first witness"

He called Trooper Manchester.

Manchester marched stiffly up the aisle and took his place on the witness stand. The courtroom was so quiet I could count my heart beats and hear the air surge in and out of my lungs.

"Trooper Manchester, you were the officer who placed this girl, Lily Ann Rose, under arrest are you not?"

Trooper: Yes sir, I am.

Lawyer: And for what charge did you take her into custody and lock her up in a cold jail cell for sixty hours where she was not allowed to call to her family or an attorney?

Trooper: Lewd and lascivious conduct, sir, in a club of questionable morals.

Lawyer: You say my client was acting in a lewd and lascivious manner.

Trooper: Yes sir, in my estimation, that's how she was acting.

Lawyer: Trooper Manchester, you appear to be a man of great moral character. Have you ever been to a nude beach or seen ladies in these new type two-piece bathing suits?"

Trooper: No, sir I most certainly have not!

Lawyer: Have you ever been to Hawaii and seen a hula dancer?

Trooper: No sir I have not!

Lawyer: Trooper Manchester, have you ever been to a burlesque show in the Old Howard or the Casino, or anywhere?

Trooper: No sir, I would not!

Lawyer: Trooper Manchester, have you ever seen Mae West in a movie?

Trooper: No sir, I have not!

Lawyer: Well if you've never seen a nude woman, have never seen a girl in two-piece bathing suit, have never seen a Hawaiian hula dance, have never seen a burlesque show, nor a Mae West movie, then how in the world can you judge what is or is not lewd and lascivious. Your honor, because we only have this man's opinion as to whether or not my client was behaving in a lewd and lascivious manner, I ask that this case be dismissed for lack of evidence.

The judge reflected on this for a moment then slammed down his gavel and yelled, "Case Dismissed!"

The courtroom went wild – yelling and cheering for Lily Ann Rose.

Aunt Lillian walked proudly out of the courtroom holding my hand. "What do you think you'll do now Lily Ann?" She asked.

"Well, I know one thing. After my frightening experience in Chicago last winter and now this terrible thing, I have to conclude that maybe burlesque isn't for me. I've had some time to think these last few days and I figured I'd have to be a lot tougher than I am to put up with this life any more. Maybe I'm just not cut out to be a star.

"Good thinking, Lily."

"And I remembered that when Miss Griswold visited me the other day she reminded me of the play I had written when I was in sixth grade, and she thinks I have some talent for writing. Okay. That's it. I will be a writer."

Aunt Lillian put her arms around me and hugged me tightly as we walked out of the courthouse.

Epilogue

The years passed all too quickly from the depression era of the 1930's to the twenty-first century. It would take two or three more sequels to fill in all that happened to me in the seven decades of my life which has come so far from the life Lily Ann Rose knew that when I look back I see her only as a precious instrument that had a part in forming who I have become. I love Lily Ann Rose and respect her dreams and all she attempted to do in her lifetime. I am happy for her successes and cry for her disappointments. But above all, she always picked herself up and went on even though it meant getting knocked down again. I speak of Lily Ann Rose in the third person now, fifty-years later, because it seems as though she was another person.

Margie married her fourth husband, Clicker Joe, and lived a happy and alcohol free life for a short while but became dependent on prescription drugs, painkillers, morphine and heroine substitutes. Her husband was devoted to her until she died in her sleep in May of 1953. A book by David Kruh, *Always Something Doing*, takes a look at Boston's Infamous Scollay Square. In it Clicker Joe is described as the most famous audience member of the Old Howard Theater. And that he was. He was Margie's greatest fan, and unless he was at work, he never missed a show. He had lost an arm in an industrial accident during World War II, and was unable to applaud. So he held a clicker in his left hand which was loud enough to resound throughout the Old Howard Theater. The comics loved him also because of his loud, contagious laugh, and he laughed long at every line. Three months after Margie died, their son died in a car accident. Clicker Joe survived his family by only a few short years. Aunt Karin died tragically when her apartment house burned down in 1967. A young man of twenty-one also died attempting to save her. My wise old Granny departed this life in 1959 at the age of 89. Aunt Lillian lost her devoted husband, Pasquale De Benedictis, my Uncle Pat, in 1955. Uncle Sam followed in 1968. Sally Keith died in 1967.

As for me, I kept falling in love with love and entered and exited two tragic marriages. But I am happy to say out of these two marriages came four beautiful children who gave me something to live and work for.

In 1965, I was the wife of a navy chief stationed in Morocco. I worked as a feature writer on the base newspaper and wrote my first feature story. At that time I also had my own show on Armed Forces Radio – the Woman's Page – which was a favorite on AFRTS Spain Morocco Network. I was on my way to becoming a journalist when I returned with my children to the United States in 1968 anxious to get out of an unhappy and abusive marriage. That year, at the age of 35, Lily Ann Rose grew up and Lillian Kiernan Brown was born.

Jim Brown, my present husband and hero, had everything to do with that. I didn't know what love was until I met him. He gave me and my four children love, understanding, hope, and stability. Without Jim's deep love and understanding this book would not have been possible. Aunt Lillian loved Jim Brown too. She encouraged me to keep him in my life and was the guest of honor at our wedding. Jim even insisted she come with us on our honeymoon.

After their retirement, Aunt Lillian and Uncle John moved to Florida and lived in our second home until their death. Uncle John died in 1994 and Aunt Lillian in 1996.

As for me, I have been a columnist for the New York Times and an award winning journalist. I am a mother of four and grandmother of seven, and am working on a belated college degree. I plan to continue to write until my final curtain.

About the Author

Lillian Kiernan Brown is a writer living in Fleming Island Plantation, Florida where she writes for several publications. As a writer, a journalist, and a radio show host for Armed Forces Radio, she has traveled around the world. Her work has won many awards, but she never lost her love for Boston, burlesque, vaudeville and show business. In 1996 she was awarded the Best Actress Award for her portrayal of Flo in 'The New Girl.' Although many of her stories and photos have won many awards, her heart remains at home with her husband of 25 years, Jim Brown. Together they have raised a family of five children and she now regards being grandmother to seven children her greatest accomplishment.

CPSIA information can be obtained
at www.ICGtesting.com
Printed in the USA
FFOW04n1034021117
41783FF